shaping
the church's
ministry with youth

# shaping the church's ministry with youth

**DAVID M. EVANS**

revised edition

**JUDSON PRESS** ® VALLEY FORGE

SHAPING THE CHURCH'S
MINISTRY WITH YOUTH

Copyright © 1965
Revised © 1977
Judson Press, Valley Forge, PA 19481

Sixth Printing, 1977

Except for the articles mentioned below, the material in this book
was originally published as a series of articles in the *Baptist
Leader*.

A Letter to a Potential Christian Disguised as a Hood, *by Joseph
Wilson was originally published in* The Agitator, *a youth
publication of the Ashland Federated Church, Ashland,
Massachusetts. Used by permission.*
Alec Wants to Know, *by William W. Finlaw. From* Baptist
Leader, *February, 1965.*
Notes on a Youth Ministry *by Joseph Wilson. From* Baptist
Leader, *January, 1965.*
Touch a Teenager, *by Sharon Ballenger, adapted from* The
Christian Home, *June, 1975. Copyright © 1975 by Graded Press.*
Youth and the Church, *by Thomas Nielsen. From* Baptist
Leader, *December, 1975.*
Leader Profiles, *by Ann Carrier. From* Youth Leadership,
*October, November, December, 1973. © Copyright 1973 The
Sunday School Board of the Southern Baptist Convention. All
rights reserved. Used by permission.*
Adolescents Look at Family Clusters, *by Margaret M. Sawin.
From* Baptist Leader, *February, 1974.*
The Role of an Adult Leader of Youth, *by Gary Barmore. From*
Baptist Leader, *January, 1976.*

International Standard Book No. 0-8170-0342-8
Library of Congress Catalog Card No. 65-22676
Printed in the U.S.A. ⊕

dedicated
to the memory of my dad,
DAVID J. EVANS
1899-1962

# contents

CONTENTS (continued)

# by way of
# introduction

Alert, sensitive people always wonder about the world in which they live. They recognize social change and feel its impact. They resist, adjust, accommodate, and/or accept as they evaluate change for its good and not-so-good contributions.

They also examine society's institutions. How do institutions respond to social change? Which ones create change? Which respond creatively? Which are slow to change? Which are stabilizing forces in changing times?

Christian people are particularly interested in the church's response to social change. Such concern in the 1950s and 1960s was realized in what is known as the renewal of the church. What is the church—What is its mission—How is its mission faithfully implemented?—were important questions with which professionals and lay people wrestled. New ministries of many forms were created in an attempt to make a faithful witness and response to the rapid social changes of those years. Not the least of these new forms found expression in denominational youth departments and within the youth organizations and programs of churches.

These are still important questions, even though times are different and change seems less dramatic, or at least less turbulent.

Sensitized by the civil rights movement, the battle for equal rights and opportunity seemed at one time a struggle between whites and blacks, the internal affairs of certain nations, particularly the United States. Sensitized by developing third world nations, concern now about equal rights and opportunity is today continental and global. The conflict over Asian nations and boycott of the majority of African nations at the 1976 Montreal Olympics is but one illustration. The growing voice and influence of these nations in the United Nations is another.

Sensitized in recent years by women's consciousness, the equal rights and opportunity battle today involves male and female. The battleground includes not only public facilities and jobs but private homes and family life-style as well. The issue can be very personal for the "haves" as well as the "have-nots" as increasingly busy pastoral, family, and other counselors know.

What is the church? What is its mission? How does it implement its mission? These are important questions always. The answer includes advocating change when it seems necessary. It also means giving support when change is hard and seemingly too much with which to cope. It results in the church creating issue-oriented groups at one time, personal support groups at another; biblical/reflection groups here, parenting and drug abuse/misuse groups there; world hunger task forces for some, spiritual hunger groups for others.

*Shaping the Church's Ministry with Youth* centers in on these questions as they relate specifically to youth. The ideas are the result of intimate association with many youth and adults. Read and discuss it, recognizing that the church has an opportunity unique among institutions. The church's mission is unique. It is also unique that youth believe in and look to the church at the very time they are suspicious and distrustful of most other institutions.

## concerning its use

Each chapter is concluded with several questions for the reader's consideration. These are provided to stimulate thinking and to encourage discussion. They are not meant to be a complete coverage or review of the chapter. Let the suggested questions be a guide for developing other questions. An appendix is provided in the back of the book as an additional resource for the study of the chapters. Reference is made to this material from time to time in the question section.

The use of the book is suggested among adults concerned with the church's youth ministry: pastors, Christian education directors, church school teachers and youth counselors, parents, youth committee personnel, and Christian education board members. Youth, likewise, especially thoughtful senior highs, will find it helpful. It might be possible to create meetings of adults and youth to consider portions of the book, such as the chapter, "Four Kinds of Youth." One cannot be sure which age group is the most empathetic or most threatened by the different kinds. One's insight will be enlarged if discussions can include persons who are not identified with the church.

Several settings are possible, such as five two-hour sessions. One church used the text for one of its ten-week Sunday church school electives for adults. Groups of parents have met to read and talk during youth meetings. All settings are possible for local churches and for groups or associations of churches.

However the book is used, these things are urged: First, let there be adequate time for reading and studying the chapters. Reading can be done on an individual basis or several persons could take turns reading aloud while group members follow the reading in their books. Second, let there be ample time for discussion at the point of meaning for the real situation in which the group lives, as well as at the point of basic theory. Third, let there be good leadership, individual or team, youth or adult.

## concerning the content

*Shaping the Church's Ministry with Youth* was first published in 1965. It was written near the conclusion of what American Baptist Churches called The Youth Evaluative Study, a four-year program directed by the Department of Ministry with Youth of the American Baptist Board of Education and Publication during the years 1961—1965. Much of the content was first delivered at the Pastor's Convocation, Sioux Falls College in South Dakota, January, 1964. It was later evaluated by youth and adults in several settings before appearing as monthly articles for *Baptist Leader.*

The invitation of Judson Press to update it is much appreciated. The suggestions from youth program personnel in the Division of Church Education of the American Baptist Board of Educational Ministries have been most helpful. Thanks are due those persons who are authors of the resources in the appendix for permission to include their material. Now, as originally, *Shaping the Church's Ministry with Youth* intends to encourage churches to take a new and fresh look at their ministry with and among the young—youth's involvement in the church's ministry, youth's leadership in and response to the churches.

It is of personal significance to the author to acknowledge that the once young parent of preschool and elementary school children, David Trevor, Janel, and Bronwyn, now in college and senior high school, first wrote the book as if youth were all "he," none "she." They, with Grace, have been helpful reminders that God is much more than a "he." Change is for real.

# the struggle
# for an authentic ministry

YOUTH WORK IS COMPARATIVELY YOUNG. H. H. Muchov in *Jugend und Zeitgeist (Youth and the Spirit of the Times)* pinpoints its start in 1770 with the beginnings of student associations, saying that "a younger generation only then shows a face of its own, when it does not share any longer the same spiritual space with the older generation." Commenting on the effect of the early days of the Industrial Revolution upon students, A. H. van den Heuvel says: "It was the young generation which first paid the price of technological progress: the experience of the parents was not any longer normative for them. The invisibility of the fathers' profession diminished their influence on their sons. The new problems of urbanization and collectivization were perhaps already known to the parents but had not yet had the time to penetrate into the schools and all other spheres of life." [1]

Prior to this time "youth" did not exist. One was a child or an adult. With the Industrial Revolution, Western society lost this stability, and youth became dissatisfied with unchanged lessons in a changing society. Ferment among youth has continued.

[1]"The New Situation in the West," *The Ecumenical Review,* January, 1963, pp. 157, 163.

## emergence of the youth fellowship

Post-1770 church history is dotted with periods of ferment by and about the young. One of these occurred as recently as the 1930s and early 1940s. Out of this period of ferment came the concept of the youth fellowship—a concept which has dominated the thinking of many denominational youth departments, and which will undoubtedly remain as a part of the vocabulary of the local church for some years to come.

Concerning the pre-youth fellowship era, Dr. Oliver deWolf Cummings, a onetime director of youth work says:

> Before the development of the Youth Fellowship, a state of affairs existed in the churches which was quite chaotic. Several organizations competed for the loyalty of youth with overlapping functions, gaps unprovided for, and with limited coordination. Wherever a new need arose, a new organization was developed—with a limited objective, but usually with a full quota of officers and committees.
>
> The church youth program in Ourtown looked like this. We had the Sunday church school, with its organized youth classes (using such class names as Baraca, Philathea) . . . the Sunday evening "young people's society," with separate officers . . . the missionary organizations for girls, and in some denominations, for boys . . . also the Boy Scouts, Girl Scouts, Camp Fire Girls, Hi-Y, athletic clubs, and many others. And often the cooperation between all these separate organizations was very poor.
>
> Gradually, a simpler and more effective approach of the church to its youth work was discovered. In one denomination after another, steps were taken to establish an improved organizational pattern—the Youth Fellowship. In these developments, young people themselves, lay leaders of youth, ministers, and national officials have had a part. *Now, a new force, the Youth Fellowship movement, is abroad in America, and the end is not yet.*[2]

The "big idea" behind the youth fellowship movement was the emphasis on fellowship, which was interpreted to mean "a spiritual experience of individuals and of a group." The Youth Fellowship arose out of a philosophy of Christian education which emphasized "(1) the central place of the church as a true broth-

[2] *The Youth Fellowship* (Valley Forge: Judson Press, 1956), pp. 16, 17.

erhood of Christian community, and (2) the sacredness of human personality as over against an excessive stress upon organization."[3]

Those who experienced the birth of the youth fellowship in the early 1940s said that fellowship is essential for human beings, "whether as early adolescents . . . arriving at a conscious awareness of their need for group associations or as later adolescents . . . alert to problems of social adjustment." They advocated that the youth fellowship provide such fellowship as well as "be the expression of the highest relationship for which the church exists—man's spiritual association with God and with his fellows."[4]

## continued unrest about youth work

About the time *The Youth Fellowship* was published in 1956, a new unrest emerged out of "an excessive stress upon organization." All around were evidences of social change with its accompanying "problems of social adjustment." With it also came "a conscious awareness" of the need of association—spiritual and human—which had been lost in the concern for organization.

The conviction that persons took priority over organization and activity was not very evident. Constitution writing consumed much time for staff and other adults and youth identified with national church youth organizations. States, associations, and local churches were encouraged to pattern constitutions similarly. The youth fellowship became known as a churchwide organization for all young people ages twelve through twenty-four—junior high, ages twelve through fourteen; senior high, ages fifteen through seventeen; older youth, approximately ages eighteen through twenty-four. Church publishing houses created resources especially designed to meet the needs of each age group. Organizational and group leadership manuals were printed in abundance. During that "organizational" period, a schism

[3]*Ibid.*, p. 17.
[4]*Ibid.*, p. 19.

developed between "youth" and "student" workers, leading to the
then distinction between youth fellowship and student movement.
Organizational efforts toward fellowship resulted in something
other than fellowship.

## quest for renewal

Tired of "playing church," denominations and ecumenical
church youth bodies held national and regional gatherings to seek
the renewal of the youth fellowship, if indeed, not the renewal of
the church. They sensed that the popular understanding of "fellowship"—a good time and a good feeling—was not *koinonia,* the
Greek word most frequently used in the New Testament to mean
Christian fellowship. They were impressed with its emphasis on
being "members of one another." Youth's commitment to the
church was real. They were all concerned about what was
happening in the world. One young person wrote in preparation
for an American Baptist Ministry with Youth Consultation:

> In this world of revolutions, expansions, and uncertainties, youth
> have found themselves caught in a web of subtle idolatry and
> frustrating anxiety. Thanks to Sputnik and the Project Argus, they
> have been shocked into the realization that all is not right with the
> world. They live in the midst of tension and change. They are part of a
> world that is capable of committing racial suicide in a few short hours of
> nuclear warfare.
>
> The piercing realization to which Christian youth have come is that
> they are inescapably a part of this "mess." The concept of the sinfulness
> of man has come to have new meaning for them; and they view it in the
> symbols of the atom and ballistic missile rather than the forbidden
> apple of the tree of knowledge.
>
> Through the sufficient grace of our Lord, however, Christian young
> people are not defeated, nor are they dismayed. They do not attempt to
> escape the realism and terror of human failure through the youthful
> expressions of "rock 'n roll" or "beat generation" philosophy. They do
> not sit in fear awaiting human extinction by radiation fallout. They are
> not on the grandstands merely existing and hoping for a change toward
> the better.

To the contrary, the gift of the Holy Spirit has emboldened the Christian youth to affirm that God still commands the universe. There is still justice and mercy in the world. They continually call to remembrance that Christ died for men of all ages, their own included. The cross, with its message of redemption and reconciliation for all men who believe and act, still towers over the mushroom cloud of the hydrogen bomb.

This is the message that the church must impart to the world—in word and deed. The church needs to be renewed, and the Baptist Youth Fellowship longs to be the instrument which will, in part, bring "her bud to glorious flower."

## continued social unrest

The concern and spirit which motivated that period reshaped the thrusts of most national church bodies, denominational and interdenominational publishing houses and, of course, many local churches. The era in which Christian education was done through youth organizations was largely over.

More important, however, than all the interpretations of what had happened, new emerging concepts, patterns, and vocabulary, was the continuing impact of the changing cultural situation.

Violence surged in Southeast Asia and the Middle East, as it did in racially changing neighborhoods. Assassinations of political and social movement leaders were sobering. The voting age was lowered from twenty-one to eighteen, as was the drinking age in many areas. The drug scene grew, spreading from ghettos to suburbs, streets to campus housing. Birth control became available to the young, as well as to their parents, significantly changing attitudes and behavior about premarital and extramarital sexual relations. Dissolving marriages and breakup of family structures continued. Young men and women began moving into living relationships without wedding ceremonies. Women's consciousness and liberation was real and mind boggling to many.

At the same time, the political and social unrest of the late 1960s and early 1970s was followed by a period of turning inward. The social activism of many churches took a back seat to such new concerns as transactional analysis and parent effectiveness training. Offspring of parents and grandparents who long ago had abandoned the church's midweek prayer service were now into transcendental meditation and other Eastern religious influences. Churches that tended to be more tolerant and responsive to social change found their voices getting less of a hearing in favor of the more direct, simplistic, secure orthodoxy of fundamentalism. The appeal of the charismatic movement to the young grew. The sounds of guitars and rock combos accompanied the gospel story in "Godspell," "Jesus Christ Superstar," and in Leonard Bernstein's "Mass." The warmth, enthusiasm, joy, and informality of countercultural expressions of the church illustrated once again how the experience of the parents was no longer normative for the young.

### "new occasions teach new duties"

Needless to say, stability has not been and is not today a characteristic of our age. Little could some of us appreciate even a few years ago how fluid, mobile, and flexible churches would need to be if we were really to address ourselves to the "problems of social adjustment" and respond to the recurring need for Christian fellowship, "a spiritual experience of individuals and of a group."

Nor can we imagine, maybe not even want to, what the future calls from us. We may even fear it. "Taking a new step, uttering a new word is what people fear most," said Dostoyevsky. Change is for sure. Which means that new opportunities are for sure also. Only those who do not see new opportunities fear change.

New opportunities belong to the churches according to the 1976 Gallup Report on Religion in America. A study of young people in Dayton, Ohio, is instructive and encouraging. Dayton, considered a "barometer" or "weather vane" area for the nation, showed persons under thirty years of age to be very religious in terms of levels of belief, pro-church in certain respects, willing to work for the church if called upon, hungry for the mystical and transcendent (only a small percentage involved in Eastern religions, mysticism, yoga, and other esoteric groups), and to hold attitudes generally consistent with Judeo-Christian ideals. Prominent characteristics among the young included:

a strong desire to live a good life and an awareness of the need to grow spiritually;

sensitivity to injustice and concern over trends toward immorality in society;

eagerness for change and innovation (nothing new);

interest in a life of service (one-third of respondents said they would like to go into some kind of social work).

This seems to suggest that if we can blend youth's will to believe with their desire to help others, the church's future youth ministry is promising. Other studies show that churches which combine the two ingredients of "service" and "survival" seem to do just that—survive and serve. The Gallup study infers that "survival"—working for the church organization as an end in itself—is appropriately minimized in our ministry with youth. "Service," meeting the needs of people, can be highlighted and maximized among the young.

The materialism and apathy of churches, along with those "out of step with the times" provokes the criticism of the young, according to the study. At the same time, the church and organized religion enjoy the confidence of the young as does no other institution—military, education, government, big business, or labor.

What is more, while the percentage of people believing religion was increasing its influence on American life declined steadily from 6 percent to 14 percent between 1957 and 1970, the trend has been reversed. The 1976 study shows that 39 percent feel religion is increasing its influence. Among those who feel there is a religious awakening are youth, many of whom are attracted to new cults.

Let us take heart. The opportunity is ours if we will take it. The link between the will to believe and desire to help others is possible to implement. If we will do it, we will further encourage youth. We will involve "youth in ministry." We will increase the future effectiveness of the church's mission.

## the concept of ministry

Before proceeding, three underlying premises need mentioning:

First, much of what is said about the church's ministry with youth is person-centered rather than age-group-centered. Youth have much in common, but in the final analysis, they are individuals, not a group.

Second, the word "ministry" is not to be confused with clergy or thought of as another word for program. Ministry implies the biblical concept of ministry/servanthood (to God and others). All that is said intends to affirm this concept.

Third, ministry with youth means ministry to and by youth and to and by adults who work with youth. Specifically, it embraces (1) an adult-to/with-youth ministry and youth-to/with-adult ministry—youth and adults have knowledge, experience, faith, and service to offer which each needs—and (2) youth-to/with-youth ministry, and adult-to/with-adult ministry. Let us never underrate the essential value and power of peer groups to influence and interpret. All of which is to say that youth and adults are in the ministry together.

## FOR DISCUSSION

1. "With the Industrial Revolution, Western society . . . youth became dissatisfied with unchanged lessons in a changing society" (page 13). We live in a time of many dangers. What are the evidences of youth's dissatisfaction with what they are taught today?

2. It is suggested that in at least one period of history, organization took precedence over human personality. To what

extent is this condition currently true in our church's ministry with youth? What of our youth groupings? What of the church as a whole?

3. What ideas come to our minds when we hear the terms "youth work," "youth ministry," "ministry with youth"?

4. What are the *real* feelings of the church-related youth of our acquaintance about what the church is and does? What are the changes in feelings as one progresses from being a junior high, to senior high, to young adult?

For further reading on "new opportunities," the reader will find helpful *Religion in America 1976,* The Gallup Opinion Index, Report No. 130.

# embracing
# the concept of ministry

THE CHURCH'S MINISTRY WITH YOUTH has certain "givens." The first given is the gospel; the second, the world; the third, the person. The first is that which God has revealed to us, which we affirm and experience, and to which we witness; the second is the existential situation; the third is the development of the maturing youth. Another way of expressing it might be God at work in history, God and the person in the contemporary scene, and the person's response to the love of God.

## GIVENS OF THE MINISTRY

*1. The first given is the gospel.*

The mission of God is the redemption of the world. Christianity's history is filled with specific acts and events of God's redemptive purpose. From Abraham, Isaac, and Jacob, to the calling of Moses and the crossing of the Red Sea; from letting the people have their kings to the calling of the prophets; from the exile to the remnant; in all these events and on to the most hoped-for and climactic of all events, the birth of Christ, and his continuing life, death, and resurrection, God's love and efforts to redeem creation are witnessed.

These "many and various ways" not only reveal the fact of God's love, but also its depth. There is no one way to which God has been limited in seeking to restore rebellious human beings to fellowship with their Creator and to each other. Instead, God's mighty acts for our redemption have been characterized by flexibility. God has engaged in no "bargaining" relations—so much benefit for every good deed, and so much punishment for every evil deed. Rather, God's love has been infinite in scope. God's willingness to forgive has gone far beyond our ability to rebel and sin. This is supremely witnessed to in the Christ event and articulated forcefully by the evangelists John and Paul: "God loved the world so much that he gave his only Son. . . ." "God was in Christ reconciling the world to himself, no longer holding men's misdeeds against them. . . ."[1]

This heritage which we affirm is one of the givens of the church's ministry with youth.

*2. The second given is the world.*

The object of God's love is the world, where people are: where they are born, work, study, play, love, marry, laugh, cry, suffer, and die. Rather than stand apart from and condemn that world, God is seen in Christ as one who stands with it. Therefore, it is always "God's" world and "our" world.

And what kind of world is it? Revolution may be the word which best describes it. At the very least, it is a world of rapid social change. Urbanization, industrialization, mobility, automation, population explosion, mass communications, new explorations and findings in the natural world, political, ideological, racial, economic, and religious pluralism and revolution, not to mention sweeping changes in thought and practice concerning personal and family morality, and what some call secularization—all these mark the world in which we live. Yet, today, as at any other time in history, that world is the object of God's love, the context in which God's love and our sin clash, and therefore that world is the inevitable context of our ministry with youth.

[1] *The New English Bible.* © The Delegates of the Oxford University Press and The Syndics of the Cambridge University Press, 1961.

*3. The third given is the person.*

Complementing the changeless gospel and the changing world is the changeless yet changing development of persons: changeless in the sense that changes will inevitably take place as the person develops, and changing in the sense that we cannot be completely certain as to just when and how the changes will occur.

One of the basic struggles in which each person is engaged is the struggle for self-identity. The most critical period in the struggle is that of youth; for it is at this time that the individual takes the identity one has had as a child and the experimental and wishful identities one is experiencing in the present, and tries to bring them together into some kind of self-image. Such a "new birth of identity," as Ross Snyder expresses it, is slowly developed through failure, success, personal creativity, and interpersonal relations.

Physical growth and maturation, the loosening of family ties and acquiring of independence, the need for success with and recognition by peers, are indications of how acute this struggle for self-identity is for youth. In the process, inherited religious beliefs and practices are likely to be brought into question. Indeed, finding a style of life, responding to what God has done, is doing, and will do, involves tension and struggle between old and new values, ideas, and interpretations, so that the church's ministry with youth may well be called, in the words of Perry LeFevre, "the ministry of self-identity."

## shape of the ministry

The gospel (content) and the world (context) converge on and in the person. Thus, the three givens merge and shape the church's ministry with youth. One given without the others, or two without the third, make the ministry meaningless. To think of the gospel and the world apart from persons makes for irrelevancy. To consider gospel and persons apart from the world as persons experience it, produces the same result. And to deal with the world and the persons in it, apart from the gospel, is to impose on them a self-identity that is inadequate and ultimately false. For it is only in light of the gospel that persons can discover who they really are and what is the meaning of their existence.

Affirming that God is, that God's mission is redemptive, that God's redemptive activity focuses on people and that their response is, in part, evidenced in their struggle for self-identity, let us further affirm that those who have received Jesus Christ and have entered into fellowship with God are now the people of God, who need to identify with and take on God's mission in the world. These people are the church.

Such thoughtful writers as Hendrik Kraemer and Francis Ayres remind us that when we say the church is the people of God, or that the church is ministry, or again that the church is mission, we are actually saying the same thing. "The inner urge of God towards the world entered into the world in Jesus Christ, and through the Church this divine urge continues." [2] "The ministry of the church is the proclamation of what God has done for men and his call to answer his love with theirs. The ministry of the church is to heal the sickness in society as well as in individual souls. The ministry of the church is to work for the growth of persons in community, the development of men." [3]

In D. T. Niles' book, *Upon the Earth*,[4] we read, "The life and mission of the church is the result of the coming of the Holy Spirit into the world. Because of Him, the Church is engaged in the proclamation that Jesus is Lord. By the Holy Spirit alone is the announcement born that Jesus Christ has come in the flesh (1 John 4:2). He thrusts the Church out to make this proclamation, He empowers the Church to make it under all circumstances, He effects in the Church a demonstration of it, He gives to men the gifts of repentance and faith by which they accept the Lord who is proclaimed and confess Him."

[2]Hendrik Kraemer, *A Theology of the Laity* (Philadelphia: The Westminster Press, Copyright 1959, W. L. Jenkins), p. 32. Used by permission.
[3]Francis O. Ayres, *The Ministry of the Laity* (Philadelphia: The Westminster Press, Copyright 1962, W. L. Jenkins), p. 32. Used by permission.
[4](New York: © McGraw-Hill Book Co., 1962), p. 69.

To say church is also to say ministry. To say ministry is also to say church. The church—the people of God—participates in Christ's ministry. A group of people who call themselves a church follow Christ and participate in Christ's ministry. They are not content to be admirers of Christ. Yes, a chief characteristic of God's people is ministry, or (as we are more accustomed to saying) service. Either we as the church are Christ's servants or we are something else—not the church.

To speak of the church's ministry with youth, therefore, is to recognize that the church has ministries or various forms or acts of service, and that among these is the ministry to and of a particular person or group of persons whose experiences are related to what we identify as youth.

## goal of the ministry

The shape this ministry takes is not uniform. There cannot be a "company way" if we are to remain faithful to the flexible character of God's redemptive activity and minister relevantly in a rapidly changing world. Rather than turn to a manual or handbook to discover how to organize for ministry, a church must look to its community to discover how *it* is organized—the educational and employment patterns and opportunities of its youth, their leisure-time activities, youth's involvement in the community's crime rate, what character-building associations there are in the community, what the ratio is of youth meaningfully related to the churches as compared to those who are not—and then organize accordingly and appropriately. Such organization on the part of the church will have a dual focus— first, the ministry when the church is gathered, and second, the ministry beyond the "home base."

Every community has a uniqueness and integrity of its own. Communities, in turn, are made up of persons who have a uniqueness and integrity of *their* own. As a result, a church is compelled to have a *ministry* of uniqueness and integrity if that ministry is to be meaningful. Such a ministry will be conceived in light of and given birth to by the very flesh and blood of the community in which it is carried on. It is there that the church, by the Holy Spirit, has been set down. And it is there that persons, as they are guided by the Holy Spirit, will come to their real identity given them by God in Jesus Christ.

All this is embraced in the objective of the church's educational ministry, which, paraphrased, reads:

> The objective of the church's ministry with youth is that all youth and workers with youth be aware of God through his self-disclosure,
>> especially his redeeming love as revealed in Jesus Christ,
>>> and
>> enabled by the Holy Spirit respond in faith and love;
>>> that
> as new persons in Christ they may
>> know who they are and what their human situation means,
>> grow as sons of God rooted in the Christian community,
>> live in obedience to the will of God in every relationship,
>> fulfill their common vocation in the world,
>>> and
>> abide in the Christian hope.[5]

### FOR DISCUSSION

1. What is your understanding of the church's mission? (Before discussing this, each individual might write out a statement and share it with other members of the group.)

2. What are some illustrations of the ministry of adults to youth? of youth to adults? of youth to youth? In the church's ministry with youth, what is the ministry of adult to adult?

3. "Let us . . . affirm that those who have received Jesus Christ and have entered into fellowship with God are now the people of God, who need to identify with and take on God's mission in the world" (page 25). Is our church adequately equipping youth to do this? What is necessary for youth if they are to identify with and

[5]Based on the curriculum objective carried through the American Baptist Churches—Cooperative Curriculum Project Curriculum Design. Used by permission.

take on God's mission in the youth scene?

4. Speaking of the church's ministry with youth, the statement is made that "the shape this ministry takes is not uniform. There cannot be a 'company way' . . ." (page 26). Flexibility is stressed. An awareness of youth as persons and knowledge of the community are highlighted. It is suggested that organization for ministry is two-pronged: (1) when the church is gathered, and (2) the ministry beyond "the base." Relating these ideas to our situation, what concerns do they arouse? What might they cause us to do?

# ministry with persons

Population changes have been dramatic in the last two and three decades. The "baby boom" of the years immediately after World War II placed great pressure on elementary education in the 1950s. Many new buildings were built and additions made for public school and church and synagogue education among children.

Pressure shifted to secondary and higher education in the 1960s. A history-making 1.2 billion-dollar education bill in 1963 made significant achievements possible, such as college dormitories for several thousand students a year, many new public colleges and new buildings for engineering students and other graduate students. Seventy thousand additional students enrolled in colleges yearly through federal loan programs.

The population increased at tremendous rates. Fifteen- through nineteen-year-olds increased 17 percent during years 1963—1965. There were 4.2 million students in institutions of higher learning in 1962, 5.2 million in 1965. That same year there were thirteen million young adults, ages twenty through twenty-four, two million more than in 1960. We built. My, how we built.

It's a different picture today. While women of childbearing age birthed an average of 3.61 children in 1960, the average was

reduced to 2.43 in 1970, 1.76 in 1976. One result is that many elementary and secondary school buildings are less crowded than a decade ago. Some space goes unused. Redistricting is closing some neighborhood schools. Neighborhoods have changed. Hence, children are bused to schools in other neighborhoods.

As faculty retire, their positions are often not refilled, especially in higher education. Less money is available for graduate education. Support teachers and staff, need-based programs, and other forms of special education are cut in order to increase salaries for faculty and "essential" services. At the same time, we hear the need for more services, program, personnel, and money for senior citizens. Yesterday's attempt to respond to the increased number of young is no less than today's desire to respond to the increase in rising population of persons sixty years and older.

The ministry with youth challenge is not "bigger and bigger." It is "better and better." What does it say to churches that in 1975 the number of divorces in the United States exceeded one million? That the birthrate among middle-class teenage girls is on the increase? That one of ten adults in the United States cannot read? What does it say when the young look beyond the church for help in their inward look?

The implications and implementation of the objective: "That all persons be aware of God . . . and . . . respond in faith and love" is exciting and sobering to church and youth. Are we really committed to that objective, really ready and willing to minister?

## youth program and youth ministry

It is imperative that a church recognize the difference between an active youth program and a relevant ministry with youth. It is possible for a church—large, medium-sized, or small—to be filled to overflowing with youth engaged in many activities, yet to have such activities be largely irrelevant to the real issues with which life confronts these youth. The tragedy is that what we do ends all too often as nothing more than time-consuming, energy-devouring, feverish busyness, failing to help youth:

—to accept themselves as persons and to accept what it means to be a brother or a sister, a son or daughter;

—to learn to live with their bodies in a body conscious society— sexually and medically; consider a variety of values and pressures about sex and drugs and decide how they will use and allow their bodies to be used;

—to resolve the conflict between their desire and need for independence and their longing for the recognition and acceptance which come from interdependence;

—to fathom the mystery of the church as "one body in Christ," yet live in communities where there are churches of many denominations;

—to meet the disillusionment of church polities, tensions, and divisions;

—to be nurtured through their period of idealism and faith, and to feel accepted and loved through their period of skepticism and doubt, cynicism and unbelief;

—to discover the joy and challenge of living in a world in which there are many religions, creeds, races, and cultures;

—to know the joy of freedom and the responsibilities that go with it;

—to channel their sense of justice and desire "to be of service," yet not risk involvement which might impair their relationship with friends and family;

—yes, to minister to their need "to work out in fear and trembling" their "own salvation."

There is a significant difference between an active youth program and a relevant ministry with youth. It is, of course, possible for a church to have both. But, because it is much easier to conduct a busy program and administer an active organization than to serve the needs of persons, we often settle for the program and the organization, forgetting about the needs of the person.

## principles for shaping the ministry

If it is true, as we have affirmed, that the spirit of the gospel must characterize our church's ministry, and that the community in which our churches are set down determines the shape of that ministry, then it follows that it will be impossible for all of us to agree on the exact shape of our churches' ministry with youth. We can, however, cite some principles to guide us in shaping the church's ministry with youth.

The following two principles are concerned with the sacredness and importance of the person:

1. *The church's ministry with youth is with youth as persons and not solely as an age group.*

One may generalize when speaking of youth. They are passing through a period of great decision making—decisions about faith, about work, about a mate. They have many struggles—about adult authority, acceptance by peers, living with oneself, and relationships with the other sex. With these concerns of youth in mind, our churches plan peer-group exposures out of which, it is hoped, meaningful experiences and relationships will result. The tremendous influence of the peer group and the value and necessity for youth to have peer-group experiences are beyond question. Many significant experiences will take place in and as a result of a group experience.

And yet we deceive ourselves when we think that by providing classes, groups, and activities for youth, we are doing everything. Youth need and want groups, but to limit ourselves to group ministry is to limit our ministry. This is dramatically illustrated when a fifteen-year-old girl reports she is pregnant, or when an eighteen-year-old boy, in a fit of anger, kills his father.

The church, or any other group, is not necessarily at fault when something like this happens. Nevertheless, the fact remains that a good group experience may not get "inside" the life of a troubled person in the group. Our group discussions may never get at the tremendous loneliness of the boy whose dad, a real pal, has recently died; or at the hostility of the fourteen-year-old girl who would rather be living with her father, who is divorced from his wife, than with her mother. The senior high teacher may be frustrated because he is unable to make life after death meaningful to Joe, when Joe is even more frustrated because of his uncertainty about life after high school graduation.

Our failure to minister to the person was brought home to me when, as pastor, I invited a sixteen-year-old girl to become a member of the church. During a six-month period she had become actively involved in the church fellowship and seemed ready for membership. Her response to the invitation was, "No." Upon inquiring into her reason, I learned the story of her background— that when she was a baby, her mother had died; and that her father, with a drinking problem and many "wives," had not accepted responsibility for her or her brothers and sister.

Despite the good care of concerned persons, the girl did not know a normal mother-daughter relationship. One of the results of this was what might be interpreted as an occasional "wild streak." Some persons, and particularly certain parents, were concerned, therefore, about relationships with the girl. She was aware of this concern, as was I. In discussing it with her, I tried to point out that I thought she was taking this more seriously than were other people. I proceeded to point out that she was worthy of church membership regardless of what certain people thought of her. Together with mentioning her good participation in the discussions of the senior high church school class and her leadership at youth fellowship meetings, I indicated that the requests for her to sing solos in the youth choir and senior choir were indications that she was wanted. I made a strong case over her musical involvement, whereupon she replied, "But I don't want to be liked because I can sing; I want to be liked because of who I am."

Our church of 180 members had, on the average, fifteen junior high and senior high youth involved in the Sunday activities. As one who had been nurtured in the Baptist Youth Fellowship and had been involved in leadership roles on local church, association, state convention, and national convention levels, I knew the standards of the BYF. I also had the "know how." As a pastor,

Christian education was one of my primary concerns. And yet, despite the right emphases and committees, our youth group work, small as it was, did not minister to the real needs of at least one person. It related to this particular girl on a superficial level. It failed to give her a sense of belonging.

Though group ministry is valid, our ultimate concern for youth is not for youth as a group. Rather, youth are to be viewed as persons who are made in the image of God and for fellowship with God, and as sinners who are beneficiaries of God's redemptive act in Jesus Christ. They are unique individuals involved in many relationships of varying depth with persons of all ages, and for whom the meaning of the gospel is fully realized only when the church ministers to them as persons caught up in these relationships.

When a church says that it is too small to have a youth program, it says more about its concept of ministry than about its size. To hear adults ask, "How can we hold our young people?" or to hear youth ask, "How can we get more kids to come?" or for all of us to be anxious about a "more interesting class" or "better meetings"— all these indicate worthy concerns. But for these to become predominant suggests that people are not being motivated to ask the most important questions.

The size of a church, the number of its youth, or the complexity of the church's activities cannot be the sole factors for judging the church's ministry with youth. Indeed, the church having only one known young person has a ministry with youth. This person has a wide field of relationships, all of which challenge his and her response in faith and love. Encouraging and supporting this response, and uniting even one person in a meaningful way to the life and mission of the church, are a part of the church's test of faithfulness.

2. *"The wide field of relationships" suggests another principle, namely, that the church's ministry with youth is to the whole person.*

The thirteen-year-old girl, wondering if she will "ever fill out," does not stop wondering when she enters the church building. The sixteen-year-old car enthusiast does not suddenly put his hot rod in the back of his mind when the pastor announces the call to worship. The couple in college who have had intercourse may need to be "anxious about tomorrow."

It seems trite to suggest that we are all "full gospel" Christians, that we believe in the whole gospel. It further seems unnecessary to point out to Bible-reading Christians that the Bible is filled with illustrations of God's awareness of the whole person—of all of life. We do so, though, in order to emphasize the truth that the church's ministry with youth must be characteristically comprehensive; it must be aware of and alert to youth's entire field of relationships; it must be concerned with the whole person. As the gospel intersects every area of life, so the church's ministry must intersect every relationship.

We have heard this idea many times. Our usual response is, "Great stuff!" However, when we illustrate what this means, many of us back down, or we say, "Our people wouldn't accept this," or "That wouldn't work in our church." For the principle that our ministry is concerned with the whole person requires that we meet people where they are; and that is hard. Taken to the next logical step, this suggests that a church may find itself engaged in activities which have heretofore been considered secular; and that is even harder.

A good book written several years ago about ministry with youth was Kilmer Myers' *Light the Dark Streets*. It was the account of how the Lower East Side Mission of Trinity Parish, New York City, tried to understand persons in terms of the totality of their lives, and in so doing, minister to all areas of their living so they might find the meaning of the gospel for their human situation. Father Myers says,

> It is true that much that is done by our youth and adults could take place as easily in a settlement house or community center. There is, however, a certain plus about the life of our mission on Henry Street. It is difficult to put into words the nature of this added factor. Perhaps

because the Church—acting unashamedly *as* Church—does all this, our communal life seems to be different. At any rate, a dimension often new, and unknown to the secular agency, is recognized—man is approached and understood as a total being.[1]

Assuming that our churches are committed to a relevant ministry with youth and to approaching each youth "as a total being,"[2] what might this principle mean?

One church, surveying its community in preparation for a vacation church school, found a group of unchurched boys. Asking them what kind of program they would like to have, the boys responded: "Teach us how to cook." Here, it developed, were boys from broken homes. Living with working mothers, they had to get their own meals and were tired of eating hot dogs and hamburgers.

Another church, knowing that the young people in its community and its own membership were the last to be hired and the first to be fired, not only developed a highly organized recreational program to occupy the time of the unemployed but also created its own employment agency.

Still another church, situated in a community where the driving habits of some of the teen-agers were a real hazard to the safety of its citizens, created a hot-rod club.

A major hurdle facing those of us who wish to implement a ministry which embraces the whole person is the struggle of emancipating ourselves from a heritage which divides life into "religious" and "secular." The struggle itself is too big for this discussion. All we can now do is take note of the problem, which, for many churches, is illustrated when people turn their backs on some phases of life and say that the purpose of the church is to strengthen the spiritual life. This is only half the truth. Indeed, it is a pious cliché which in the final analysis is unfaithful to the biblical picture of you and me and God's dealings with us.

[1]New York: Seabury Press, © 1957, and Doubleday & Company, Dolphin Books, 1961, pp. 23-24. Reprinted by permission.
[2]See "Alec Wants to Know" in the Appendix.

Life is either religious or secular, depending on one's framework of reference. If it is religious, then it is based on the admittedly risky affirmation of St. Augustine, "Love God and do as you please." If we accept the fundamental truth of the Christian faith that Jesus Christ is Lord and Savior, then we are free—free to think, to act, to be the kind of persons God has called us to be; and a youth is free to be a person. It follows that the church is free—free to meet youth where they are, to minister to their whole being and, by the Holy Spirit, to enable them to live meaningfully and creatively in every area of life as one conformed to Jesus Christ.

If the church does not embrace and seek to minister to the whole person, then the church can hardly expect the person to be a Christian "the whole time."

## FOR DISCUSSION

1. What is the difference between "an active youth program" and "a relevant ministry with youth?" In what way does the difference speak to our church?

2. What are some of the positive by-products if emphasis is placed on youth as persons? What are some of the risks?

3. What does this emphasis say to a church in terms of securing and developing leadership?

4. On page 34, we read, ". . . people are not being motivated to ask the most important questions." Assuming that this statement is true, what are the most important questions?

5. In considering "ministry to the whole person," the chapter indicates that a major hurdle to overcome is dividing life into "religious" and "secular." The consequence of this is illustrated in the chapter's last paragraph. How does this stack up with our discussion of question 3 of the chapter, "Embracing the Concept of Ministry"?

"Alec Wants to Know" and "Touch a Teenager!" are good resources for considering "Ministry with Persons." (See Appendix.)

# the younger laity

WE OFTEN HEAR PERSONS SPEAK with sincerity and enthusiasm for and on behalf of a good "youth program" with the phrase, "Youth are the church of tomorrow." There is some truth in this statement—if the person making it is speaking in the context of the organized church. As an organization, the church needs mature and experienced persons in positions of leadership. Usually, this will result in adult leadership. What is more, the interests and concerns of youth and adults will most often result in having adults assume the administrative leadership of the church. Thus, youth are the church of tomorrow.

If, however, we affirm that the church is the people of God— laity—and that they are to witness, then youth, as well as children and adults, are the church of *today*. Indeed, an examination of the nature and mission of the church shows that this "church of tomorrow" orientation is patronizingly benevolent and theologically indefensible. Persons are a part of the church by virtue of their response to God's calling. Thus, the gathered church experiences of the people of God must necessarily engage youth in witness right *now,* not in witness (or, even more parochial, in churchmanship) *tomorrow.*

The time is past when we dare think that the purpose of the church's youth program is merely to induct youth into the Christian fellowship and to get them ready for responsible roles in the life and work of the church. From the theological perspective, it is strange that we ever came upon such a viewpoint. Baptism affirms that one is united with Christ and his church, with God and mission. In the church and mission there are no second- and third-class citizens. We cannot divide persons into those who are "prepared" and those who are "getting prepared," and put the adults in the former and youth in the latter. All persons who have responded to God's call to be identified with the church are "prepared." They are ready for witness. At the same time, they are in need of continuing preparation for responsible participation in witness.

Current events are helping us to see that while many adults seem to be still at the "getting prepared" stage for witness, many youth are fully "prepared." Their involvement in the peaceful and violent liberation movements overseas and their participation in certain national human rights causes suggest that many consider themselves full members of the human race.

It can be argued, and correctly so, that many youth are involved in such activities without knowledge and understanding; that they are simply caught up in the excitement. Such is also true of many adults, which is to say that persons of all ages profane causes, and the causes suffer.

Beulah, a fifteen-year-old "marcher" of the early 1960s from Williamston, North Carolina, was visiting us in Philadelphia. As we passed the Philadelphia Museum of Art where several scenes of the movie *David and Lisa* were taken, I asked: "Did you see the movie *David and Lisa*?" "No," she responded, "the theaters in Williamston are segregated and so we boycott them." Here was one young person for whom the protest was no lark. It brought change and fuller membership in society. Consciousness raising activities help protestors and protested against to gain a fuller realization of their humanness.

Voting in public elections is one way youth exercise their full rights and privileges of citizenship. Regrettably, a large percentage of eighteen- to twenty-one-year-olds are not voting. This privilege is sometimes denied youth in churches. Some churches do not keep up with religious corporation laws, and hence deny youth full rights and privileges within the church.

What can we do, then, to say to the younger laity, "You are the church *now;* the church needs you *now*"?

## nurture oriented to "now"

First, the church's nurture must be "now" oriented. Youth must be accepted for what they are now, as well as for what they can and will become. Their preparation for witness must be within the framework of life as they experience it today—in classroom, laboratory, gym, drive-in and pizza shop, dating, driving, and in all else that is considered a part of "youth culture." Yes, they need preparation for living tomorrow, but the not-to-be-forgotten fact is that they are living now. Their real preparation for tomorrow will come when tomorrow arrives. Significant witness tomorrow will come if today's focus is on today. The gathered church experience of youth must prepare them for *now,* encourage witness *now,* and be supportive of witness *now.*

## full membership "now"

Second, youth must be accepted as full members of the church today, not as members in training. They are entitled to this position by virtue of their baptism. Even if they were not, we could ill afford the luxury of viewing the youth years as a "waiting" period. Youth need to be called upon to be themselves, not miniature adults, nor junior deacons, but the younger laity with full rights and privileges. They need to be given every opportunity for service—based upon gifts, not age; on conviction, not personality; on commitment, not experience.

Youth are in need of the maturity and experience of the older laity. At the same time, the older laity need the idealism and dreams of youth. Bringing the two groups together for across-the-generations thinking and commitment will enhance the witness of the Christian community. The church will be a more potent instrument if the older people of God will recognize the younger people of God as full members of the church—not simply as a youth organization—and will involve them in the church's life and mission *now,* recognizing that training includes not only "learning about," but also "experience in." This idea means that the church will have to wrestle intensely with such questions as these: How can the young experience most meaningfully the fellowship of the church? How can the young become involved most significantly in the service of the church? How can the young most fruitfully contribute to and participate in the structures of the church?

The answers to these questions and the manner in which youth are meaningfully and significantly involved in the fellowship, mission, and structures of the church will necessarily be based upon the "sorts and conditions" of youth and their "varieties of gifts"—even as this is the basis for the selection of more mature persons. One church, when examining its membership in terms of the tithing enlistment program it wished to undertake, selected a senior high student to be chairman. Another church, which was concerned about the curriculum materials used in its senior high division, involved several senior highs in the evaluation of materials and in the planning for their use. That youth have feelings about the way things are and ought to be in the church was indicated in a survey taken among several hundred junior high and senior high youth. The responses of the youth to the question, "What do you dislike most about your church?" was headed by their resentment over the quarreling of adults, followed closely by their dislike of "our crummy Sunday School rooms."

## implications

A discussion of the role of young people in the church often results in the question: Do you mean that youth should be on the board of trustees or deacons? If we accept gifts, convictions, and commitments as the criteria for the selection of the leadership of the church, rather than age, personality, and experience, then some youth may well assume such offices in certain churches. However, this is not the issue at stake. In truth, many youth do not wish such responsibilities and involvements. Most are content to leave these tasks to adults. What we are saying is that if youth are indeed the people of God, then this has a bearing on our attitude toward them. Rather than simply plan for them or, as sometimes happens, simply tolerate them, we shall challenge them to Christian responsibility now. Actually, by virtue of their youth, they now have energies and abilities which will not be available to them later on. To inhibit these is to run the risk of depriving the church of some significant insights, qualities, and dimensions essential to its ministry and witness.

Giving the younger laity the same rights and privileges accorded the older laity; providing them every possible opportunity for service in the life and fellowship of the church; challenging them to be full participants in the mission of God now; and expecting youth to take on the same responsibility for witness as is expected of adults—all these suggest a companion statement to one previously made. We said, "The time is past when we dare think that the purpose of the church's youth program is merely to induct youth into the Christian fellowship and to get them ready for responsible roles in the life and work of the church." The time is also past when we can forgive youth because they are youth. This is to say that youth's involvement in the great issues of our day no longer permits adults to excuse youth from accepting responsibility, blame, and judgment because they are youth. If the younger laity are to be given the full rights and privileges which they deserve, then they must at the same time be ready to accept the responsibilities which these imply and bestow. If youth are to be involved with their elders in revolution and change, they must also bear, with their elders, responsibility for the sins of the world. As Bonhoeffer said during his London period, "It could be that young people have the right to protest against the adults. But the genuineness of the protest is proved only if the younger generation knows what it means to have solidarity with the guilt of the church and to bear that burden with love, and if they themselves remain penitent in face of the word of God."[1]

This lesson the older laity must impart to the younger laity, even as many of the younger laity are seeking to impart it to their peers. It is a hard lesson. It is a difficult challenge. It is not too much to expect.

How does your church say to the younger laity, "You are the church *now;* the church needs you *now*"?

## FOR DISCUSSION

1. The section "Full Membership Now" speaks of the younger laity "with full rights and privileges." What is the real meaning of this statement?

2. Are the youth of our acquaintance able and willing to take on the same responsibility of witness as is expected of adults? If yes, illustrate. If no, why not?

3. How can the young experience most meaningfully the fellowship of the church?

4. How can the young experience most meaningfully the witness of the church?

5. How can the young experience most meaningfully the structures of the church?

[1]From an unpublished lecture.

# four kinds of youth

THERE ARE AT LEAST FOUR KINDS OF YOUTH. We may have, heretofore, thought there were only two (male and female) or three (junior high, senior high, and older youth). Yet where the church's ministry with youth is concerned, let us consider young people in terms of the following four categories.

*First, there is the young person to whom the Christian faith has meaning and for whom the gathered church experience is significant.*

This young person is responding positively to the ministry of the church and is involved in it. He is thinking through the message of the faith and teachings of the church. He may not necessarily understand everything nor accept all that the church teaches. However, he embraces what he can understand, and concerning what he does not understand he either confesses, "I don't know," or realizes that he needs more time before "this will have meaning."

In the meantime, he is participating in the life and service of the church. Through listening, talking, and working, he is growing in "the grace and knowledge of our Lord and Savior, Jesus Christ," and the relevancy of the gospel shows through his relationships in and beyond the walls of the church building. He is the kind of young person for whom we develop a strong affinity, and about whom we have some ideas or at least hopes concerning the future.

*Second, there is the church dropout.*

This youth is almost the extreme opposite of the first—"almost" because it may be that the Christian faith has meaning for the dropout and that she embraces what the church teaches. However, her experience in the church has been so meaningless, or she is so disillusioned by the contrast between the teachings and the practices of the church, that she has withdrawn from it. She is not necessarily a part of the pro-God—anti-church group and may actually love the church, but has found it necessary to separate from it, at least temporarily.

More than likely, however, neither the gospel nor the church experience has clicked with the dropout. There are many possible reasons. There may be no encouragement at home, or the encouragement of the parents may not be handled correctly. Staying home may be a form of rebellion against the folks. Possibly peer-group pressure is a factor. What goes on in church may seem unimportant, or the church may be the victim of the "so what" attitude. The teacher is a "creep" or the counselors "just aren't with it." The minister? Well. . . .

Chances are good that this young person is just bored. The programs seem irrelevant. Maybe they get too personal, or "the rest of the kids laugh when I read." Some reasons seem more genuine than others. There is real validity to many. We must hear all of them. They are saying something to us.

*Third, there is the young person for whom our ministry seems to be a kind of "holding process."*

This young person is not genuinely caught up in the message and mission of the church, while at the same time, he has not dropped out. He is neither hot nor cold. He is there, and yet he is not. The church has a good youth group, and he likes to be a part of it. He likes what the young people do. He may even be a leader. And yet, you get the feeling that he is just going through the motions.

And maybe he is! The leadership opportunities may satisfy his ego. Maybe it is his way of identifying with a "status" group, or "the right kind of people." It's a good way to get out of the house. The suppers they serve at church aren't much, but it's a change from the dorm. Besides, the programs are usually interesting. Who knows? Who can really judge? It just seems, however, that nothing of any real significance is taking place in the life of the young person.

On the one hand, it could be the program. The chances are good that this is so, for many young people are related to churches that are not interesting, nor challenging, nor worth getting excited about; neither do they excite young people about anything, not even the gospel message, let alone the gospel mission.

On the other hand, it could be the age of the persons with whom we are working. There are those who are doubtful about the possibility of much genuine response from youth. They are going through a stage of life when they are not ready to give themselves to much that is not exciting. Even among those who volunteer for ACTION, the desire to travel is high on the list of motivating reasons. So, say some, we really ought not to expect much of young people, but be content to see them through this transitory period. Perhaps all we can do is to hold them until they are ready to settle down.

Regardless of the reasons, the truth is that this young person for whom our ministry is a "holding process" causes us great anxiety. He makes us think up new ideas, tempts us to yield to attendance-increasing gimmicks, encourages us to spend more money on Cokes and potato chips, and makes us look for whipping boys to blame for our apparent failure to relate to him. So churches blame publication societies because of their poor materials, and publication societies reply that churches do not use the materials correctly.

Let's face it; there really is the young person for whom our ministry is nothing more than a holding process. (Someone has suggested that such persons make up the majority of the church membership.) This is not to suggest a *laissez-faire* approach, but if we would accept this person for what he is, we might not so frequently press the panic button over secondary matters, and might actually have more time and energy for activities that have depth and are life-changing in character. We might, hopefully, see more young people listed among those who are meaningfully and significantly related to the life and mission of the church. It could be that the young person who is merely holding on is just going through the motions because that is the standard the church has set for him.

*Fourth, there is the young person we do not even know, or if we do know her, our relationship with her is outside the church fellowship.*

She has no direct relationship to or involvement in the church's life and fellowship. Oh, she may have had as a child, but not now. She may or may not come to the church to be married.

The truth is, we do not know this young person. We see her at school and community functions together with church youth. Most of the time she dresses, acts, and talks just like the young people we do know. Once in a while she gets caught by police for shoplifting or possession of pot, like some we know. Actually, she and many like her are often not much different from the friend who is related to the church.

## implications for the church's ministry with youth

What do these young people say to us concerning the church's ministry with youth? First, their very existence suggests that the focal point of the church's ministry with youth must be persons— not programs, not groups, not institutions or traditions, but persons.

Persons call for programs and not programs for persons. Yes, a program will emerge if a principle, an idea, or a cause is to be implemented or served. The program will call for the help and service of persons. However, unless the program has a person-centered purpose for existing, it is nothing. Activities, groups, topics, and leadership roles are subject to persons living where they are and having the need for a Lord and Savior. There is no *status quo* program which churches must preserve or defend. Their program is a relevant ministry with persons in response to their call to be faithful.

Second, the very fact that these four kinds of young people exist reminds us that a church—a people of God—is a base or center of operations with a building to which many come and from which many go. Persons who come bring both good and bad tidings. Their reasons for coming are many. Their needs vary tremendously. Thus the experiences and relationships at the base must be of a quality that means something to persons. The activities and structures must speak meaningfully to young people. They must build integrity of personhood, commend the sacredness of personality, encourage the interchange of ideas and ideals, enable change of attitude and behavior to take place, enhance growth, development, and maturity, and be supportive of witness when those who share in the activities and structures are away from the security of the base.

The centralized ministry of the church must be complemented by an away-from-the-base ministry. Beyond the base, there need to be outposts or stations where a similar kind of engagement is taking place. *At these outposts or stations, the engagement is with those who cannot or will not come to the base.* The pattern or manner of engagement may be different and possibly quite foreign to that employed at the base. However, the necessity for meaningful patterns that speak to and meet young people where they are, and with which they can identify and to which they will respond, remains of the utmost importance.

Some churches are engaged in beyond-the-base ministries. A Lutheran church sponsors a coffee house in a "college town." A Presbyterian church owns a house and makes it a "drop-in" center. A Pentecostal church has a "half-way house ministry" for runaway youth. Catholic and Protestant churches finance and staff problem pregnancy telephone counseling services which often lead to personal contact. A Baptist church plans growth group experiences for its fringe youth who will not engage in worship and youth meetings at church, but who will go to someone's house to talk about life and faith.

Placing much emphasis on away-from-the-base ministries may be too much to expect of some churches. For others, it may be their ministry with youth. And for your church?

## FOR DISCUSSION

1. What is our church and what are other churches and agencies doing to minister among the several kinds of youth in our community? Where is our church strongest? Where is it weakest?

2. Are our resources and program enough of a challenge and support to those for whom the Christian faith and the church are meaningful?

3. What forces are at work—in homes, in the larger community and even in our church—which contribute to the church dropout problem?

4. Should the statement, "there really is the young person for whom our ministry is nothing more than a holding process," cause us to rethink any phase of our church's ministry with youth? Be specific.

5. What is necessary for our church to minister among the fourth kind of young person?

6. What response should we have toward homosexual and lesbian youth?

"A Letter to a Potential Christian Disguised as a Hood" in the Appendix is a good resource for discussing the church dropout and the youth we do not know. "Alec Wants to Know" also speaks to the latter. "Youth and the Church," also in the Appendix, will encourage discussion.

# flexibility and
# an atmosphere of freedom

IN THE PRECEDING CHAPTER IT WAS STATED that there are at least four kinds of young people: (1) the young person to whom the Christian faith has meaning and for whom the gathered-church experience is meaningful; (2) the church dropout; (3) the young person for whom our ministry seems to be a kind of holding process; and (4) the young person who is outside of any relationship with Christ and the church. Every church has a responsibility to all four. If we are to be faithful to our calling, it behooves the churches to discover and employ many approaches and patterns of ministry whereby all young people may be confronted with the good news and given an opportunity to respond.

As we take another look at these youth, we note that there are those who will become part of the gathered-church experience. These youth are typified by the first and third young persons listed above. Among them, of course, is the potential dropout. We also note that there are those who will not "gather" or who, at least, will not gather in conventional ways and certainly not in the church. However, let us give our attention to the former group.

## let the gathered-church experience be characterized by flexibility

*Let there be flexibility in groupings.* Should there be a group of ninth-graders who are misfits with the seventh- and eighth-graders, or with the tenth-, eleventh-, and twelfth-graders, let them create a group of their own. Should a group of two, three, or four seventh-grade boys seem to need a class for themselves, withdraw them from the coeducational experience for a while. In a couple of years, instead of hitting the girls, they will be hugging them. One year the college students and the employed older youth may have a common group. Next year, in order to meet needs, it may be advisable to create a separate group for the students. Let there be flexibility in groups.

*Let there be flexibility in the settings.* The church building and private homes are at least two possible locations for group meetings. Perhaps the college students' Sunday morning discussion group should be held on campus. There could even be two group meetings at the same time, one on campus, the other at the church building. In one church, where the eleventh- and twelfth-graders did not have any interest in a Sunday morning class, this experience was shifted to Sunday evening. Another church makes Sunday evening the major time for study, and Sunday morning the time for unstructured conversation. A third church has a seminar-type experience on Sunday morning.

For that matter, why must Sunday be the only time for meeting? One church has found it necessary to eliminate all Sunday morning peer-group experiences. The junior highs meet Monday afternoon and evening, and the senior highs on Tuesday. Sunday evenings are reserved for projects and other activities. Let there be flexibility in the settings.

*Let there be flexibility in structure.* Think of the many youth who drop out of church school during the eighth- through-twelfth-grade years. Instead of fretting over their not coming, some churches, with these youth, are engaging in six to a dozen weekend retreats throughout the year—all-day Saturday and Sunday affairs devoted to biblical and theological study. One large church, deciding that what the senior highs were doing on Sunday evening was rather "corny," divided the senior highs into five groups and decentralized into five homes. All groups were unstructured. After evaluating their experience at the end of the first year, two of the groups returned to the more traditional kind of meeting the next year. If a church wishes to provide more than one Sunday peer-group experience, let it not insist that the only way to get it is by returning to the church building. Some groups may meet at the church; others can meet at another part of town at the same time.

And while speaking of structure, let's keep organization to a minimum. Create no more organization than is necessary for getting the job done. A committee or task group can be dissolved when it has completed its work. We need to give serious thought to whether or not our organizational structures contribute to our purpose. Some organizations become the church within the church. Actually, the election of officers among status-conscious senior highs may be a real deterrent toward a redemptive fellowship. As Hendrick Kraemer says: "The institutional aspect is an indispensable apparatus which should have its due place, but not the first place; for often (though certainly not always) it is like Saul's armor for David, an encumbrance and not a help."[1]

Let there be flexibility, at least in groupings, settings, and structure, and always be prepared for change at appropriate times in order that one way of doing things may not so freeze and harden that we fail to minister to the needs of persons.

## let the gathered-church experience be characterized by an atmosphere of freedom

Our classrooms, hallways, and sanctuaries—the formal and informal, the planned and unplanned teaching-learning experiences—ought to be distinguished for encouraging curiosity and

[1] *A Theology of the Laity* (Philadelphia: The Westminster Press, 1959), p. 84. © Hendrick Kraemer. 1958. Used by permission.

inquisitiveness. Such an atmosphere sets the stage for freedom to think, freedom to be honest in what is said, freedom to be real. The opposite of this is mask-wearing and hypocrisy, giving "Sunday church school answers," saying what is expected to be said or what the teacher wants to hear, a subtle and sometimes not so subtle form of brainwashing.

*Let there be freedom to seek after truth.* Truth is the result of honest inquiry. The content of the Christian faith is no less subject to honest inquiry than is any other subject relevant to living. To deny youth all possible theories and information concerning the authorship of the Bible, which they deserve to know, is but to hinder their understanding and conviction about the authority of the Bible. What is more, it fails to prepare them for intelligent discussion and for witnessing with integrity in a pluralistic religious culture. To suggest that an analysis of jazz is out of place in the church is not only to admit to a misunderstanding of what religion is, but to admit ignorance of jazz as a medium of religious expression. To postpone the discussion of sex until after class is to postpone the facing of life itself.

One of the troublesome illustrations of what we are saying is related to books. One summer the Department of Ministry with Youth conducted three Regional Consultations on the Church's Ministry with Youth at Hillsdale, Michigan; Newton Centre, Massachusetts; and Salt Lake City, Utah. On hand were two young people and one adult from each of our state conventions and city societies.

One of the requests made to the young people was to list books they had recently read. Many kinds of books were listed, but at each consultation the same three books were always listed: *Brave New World,* by Aldous Huxley; *1984* by George Orwell; and J. D. Salinger's *Catcher in the Rye.* All three books have caused some tension for public libraries and public school systems, and even denominational youth departments. Our· purpose here is not to judge what is good reading. The point is that these books are being read.

Salinger's *Catcher in the Rye,* Kurt Vonnegut's *Breakfast of Champions,* Claude Brown's *Manchild in the Promised Land* and *Native Son* by Richard Wright are required reading in some junior high and senior high schools. If these are what youth are reading, the church needs to help young people read and consider them within the framework of the religious community, where it is hoped the young can be supported in their efforts to be transformed.

Every worker with youth should read about Holden Caulfield in *Catcher in the Rye.* He represents the need all of us have for the reconciling act of God in our lives. As unlovely as he is, Holden is representative of young people for whom Christ died and with whom the church is called to minister. Regrettably, too often this kind of youth is not in the church; in too many instances he is not wanted. Our youth program thus turns out to be an organization for nice young people, and as a result, our adults develop a limited view of youth.

*Let there be freedom to explore all of God's world.* We must be ready to acknowledge the necessity and the validity of exposing youth to differing points of view, even those which differ from our own. To be sure, it is not always necessary and important that we go out of our way to confront persons with that for which they are not ready, or of which they are not in need. To postpone such exposure, however, is to run the risk of failing to prepare persons for life. This is always a problem in our ministry with youth. Adults tend to look at youth from the perspective of their own youth. "I wasn't ready for this when I was their age." Not only has the world changed greatly since most adults were youth, but it is changing so rapidly now, and the maturation process of youth is so accelerated, that public education is upgrading subject matter yearly, continually introducing new knowledge to younger minds.

This, though, is another issue. The basic concern here is that there are no subjects, ideas, ideologies, or isms that are not subject to the Creator of life and that hence do not merit the serious examination of all Christians. The whole world is a proper subject for youth to explore. Only in such exploration can youth begin to evaluate those aspects of life which lack meaning and value. What better place than in a gathered-church experience to encourage an honest expression of doubt, a serious inquiry into the Christian faith, a real confession of sin, an uninhibited exploration of ideas, and a forthright attempt—accompanied by empathetic support— in articulating the faith? Let the gathered-church experience be, as it were, a workshop for witness in dispersion, where youth can be achievers of answers and not simply receivers of pat replies.

*Let there be freedom in the way in which youth seek truth and meaning.* An atmosphere of freedom ought also to characterize the gathered-church "style of life" or approach to the setting for the teaching-learning experience.

The *Youth Ministry Manual* of the United Church of Christ gives an illustration of this. A group of youth were brainstorming on the question, "What should the church do to improve its youth ministry?" Only positive suggestions were allowed, although some are couched in negative language. The list of replies reads like this:

"Get rid of crummy teachers." "Cut out all the emphasis on ethics." "Stress the personal relation to God." "Recognize when kids are fed up." "Have more retreats." "Discuss the real purpose of life." "Devotional materials for all the time, not just for Lent." "Explain the 'why' of the Christian religion, not just the 'whats.'" "Fellowship groups for little children." "Stuff through the week, not just on Sunday." "Seminars for older kids, instead of classes, where kids can really discuss things." "Retreats all the time, where kids really get to know each other." "Weekday Sunday school, or something." "Little groups where everybody can talk." "Talk about the real problems kids have." "Free-for-all discussion." "That morning watch idea in church, for everybody." "Emphasis on creeds, so you'd know what it's all about. At least, you'd know what you don't believe." "Get kids to participate in other church things besides just the youth stuff." "Family nights for all." "Parent-child discussion pretty often." "Training of Sunday school teachers." "Trips and things like that where you get away."

"Give kids something important to do in the church, like the adults do." "Why not have kids teach little kids?"

One boy responded like this: "Well, you know how it is at Sunday school before it starts. The kids all stand around talking about everything that's happening to them, you know. Dances maybe, or a game, or something else at school. Or maybe their parents, or their boyfriends. Well, fool them. Instead of stopping all that and saying, 'Now our class will begin,' just have them stay right where they are (sit on the floor or something) and go right on talking and teach them that way, you know."

The manual's author, Robert Dewey, comments:

"Now our class will begin" means what? What it very often means is that we will now discuss God, sin, faith, trust, love—these things and many more—in a setting completely removed from the daily experiences of the members of the class—in a safe atmosphere where everyone will behave with proper decorum ("like real Christians," we may say). Is this not often a way of avoiding those personal relationships (that personal dimension in a small group) which are, perhaps, the best vehicle we have for the communication of the gospel of Christ?

If we were to follow the boy's earnest suggestion, to let everyone sit on the floor, begin the class without an announcement to the effect that we were now beginning, and spend a good deal of time listening, would we not soon find ourselves talking with youngsters about sin, grace, trust, love, betrayal, integrity, separation, reconciliation, and the whole gamut of our concerns as Christians? In this style of approach, God might possibly find a better opportunity to disclose himself, to let his seeking love get through.[2]

Many churches work hard to have a "rah, rah," well-planned, spectacular program. It is to be observed that what is spectacular often turns out to be a dud, that those who are spectacular among the young soon learn to "play it cool," and that the unplanned often proves to be the most meaningful. Indeed, a relevant ministry with youth often calls for the discarding of our best plans.

[2]Robert D. Dewey, *Youth Ministry Manual* (Boston-Philadelphia: United Church Press, © 1963), p. 50. Used by permission.

What many youth are calling for is a more informal, "low key" approach. The implications of taking up this style of youth ministry, in contrast to "lessons" and "packaged programs," could be revolutionary for churches and publication societies.

## FOR DISCUSSION

1. How is the present grading and grouping of youth in our church helping or hindering meaningful teaching-learning experiences for all youth?

2. What percentage of our senior highs and older youth are active participants in a Sunday church school class or its equivalent? What kind of response could we anticipate if we were to consider some of the settings suggested in the section "Let there be flexibility in the settings" (page 51)?

3. Current "popular" reading books come and go. What is the current recommended bibliography of our local junior high and senior high schools and college literature classes? What is the currently popular *extracurricular* reading? Why are the young people reading the latter? Are the teachers and counselors in our church also reading them?

4. What help is it necessary to give our workers with youth in order that they may feel more confident in creating an atmosphere of freedom in our educational ministry?

For other reading read "Leader Profiles" and "Notes on a Youth Ministry," in the Appendix.

# time, size of group, and across-the-generations encounter

THE PREVIOUS CHAPTER CITED flexibility and an atmosphere of freedom as two principles that ought to characterize the gathered-church experience. Let us now consider three more principles, the first of which is an adequate quantity of time.

## time

It takes time to learn. It takes time to love. Certainly we know this. Then let us give this easily-recognized factor more serious attention. Maybe we have, and we have backed away from inevitable conclusions. Certainly if we were to act upon this as a principle for shaping the gathered-church experience, familiar patterns and some of our structures would change.

There is some evidence to support the belief that an hour (and rarely does it amount to even this much) of Sunday church school is better than nothing. Something of the Christian way of life seems to rub off. However, the real truth is that the church's educational structures do not allow time for depth study and thorough examination. The hour or less that the Sunday church school and the evening fellowship afford hardly permit persons to get started. Such limited periods of time only scratch the surface, and participants seldom become involved with vital issues.

Involvement, encounter, dialogue, engagement—words with meanings that many today are embracing—require concentration, patience, acceptance, rejection, give-and-take, talking, and listening—all of which take time. Persons with even the slightest knowledge of the ways in which groups function know that our current patterns do not and cannot permit this to happen except at a superficial level. Because of the lack of time, the best that groups seem to be able to achieve in any given session is not much more than "a good feeling." Only rarely are they able, at the next session, to pick up again where they left off. Furthermore, the moods and needs of group members change from session to session. Yet these too must be dealt with if the experience is to be a meaningful one. But if time is gone, the opportunity to deal with them may be gone too, and as a result someone may again be deprived of the "joy of salvation."

Lack of time to learn must be, in part, to blame for the great biblical illiteracy and lack of theological understanding of American youth and adults. Lack of time to love and to be loved must be, in part, the reason why so many persons fail to experience a redemptive and reconciling relationship in the gathered-church experience. The inability to internalize subject matter and the failure to implement thoughts and ideas into action, undoubtedly are related to an inadequate amount and use of time.

Let our structures be influenced by the realization that one two-hour session is more profitable than two one-hour sessions. In the church's ministry with youth we are not only concerned about imparting information, although this is an important and essential concern; we must also be concerned with setting the stage so that this information can be "kicked around" and internalized. We must provide opportunities for persons to come to grips with ideas and concepts and to see not only how they fit into a church setting, but also how they are related to all life situations. Information makes little difference if the setting in which it is given does not encourage growth and development. Our structures and patterns are not meant to be instruments for funneling information into unwilling minds. Rather, they are to be the means for helping persons change.

Some churches, facing up to the inadequacies resulting from one-hour Sunday church school classes and evening fellowship meetings, are making serious efforts to find more time. In doing so, some have added more time to their regular study periods; others have set aside special times during the week for such study. As we stated in an earlier chapter, some churches are using Sunday evenings and weekdays for major study periods rather than the Sunday morning church school hour.

Indeed, there is no one way to reschedule. Each church must find a pattern which enables it to be most faithful to its ministry with youth. Many churches may justly conclude that their present schedule is best. However, youth workers can learn much from the experience of children's workers who have a two-hour Sunday church school session, and from adult workers who are increasingly employing small study groups on Sunday evenings and on weekday mornings, afternoons, and evenings for adult education. They can also learn much from their own experiences with vacation church school, retreats, camps, and conferences, and the larger amounts of time they make available for group study and discussion. The tremendous need that young people

### EACH ARROW REPRESENTS ONE RELATIONSHIP

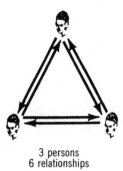 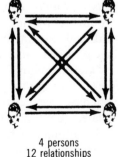 

3 persons
6 relationships

4 persons
12 relationships

5 persons
20 relationships

have to talk is sufficient reason for youth workers to find adequate amounts of time for youth to become involved in meaningful learning experiences.

What we are saying is that teaching cannot assume learning. It takes time to learn. It takes time to love.

## size of group

The size of groups and the number of persons involved should be supportive of the purpose of the experience. For singing, playing, lecturing, and viewing films, the size of the group is generally not of major significance. Although limited facilities may present a problem, fifty can usually view a film as well as five. However, if a *discussion* of the film is to be meaningful, then group size is an important consideration.

Although setting a maximum figure for the size of a group seems arbitrary and even superficial, one does need to bear in mind that the size of the group affects the number of relationships one has in a group. For example, a group of three persons has six relationships. Add one more person to the group, and there are twelve relationships, twice as many as when there was only one less person. Add one more person and there are twenty relationships.[1]

Students of this subject report that, when a group exceeds seven in number, it begins to lose its personal value; it becomes impersonal. A possible conclusion might be, then, that seven is a desirable number for study and discussion groups in which importance is attached to involvement and "meeting people where they are," such as church school classes and fellowship groups.

It has also been suggested that five is the minimum size of a group if it is to function as a group. Again, purpose is important. A meaningful exchange will transpire among only three. And, although we have often avoided groups of two, because they can be the most personal and threatening, the one-to-one conversation can have a place in the church's ministry with youth.

[1]Kenneth L. Cober, *Baptist Evening Fellowship Manual* (Valley Forge: Judson Press, 1961), pp. 15-16. Used by permission.

The realization that learning is encouraged through involvement, that the dialogical approach is more conducive to involvement than the monological approach, and that the small group lends itself to dialogue, ought not to eliminate completely the large group from the gathered-church experience. However, recognizing what has been said about time, we do have the imperative to look seriously at the purpose of the group and the best method for accomplishing that purpose.

One area in which many churches could look at their purpose and the best method for accomplishing it is the Sunday morning program. What happens during the hours set aside for the Sunday church school? We have already cited the lack of time in the church school. Yet, many churches deprive youth of study time by taking anywhere from ten to thirty minutes for an all-school or departmental general assembly, or what is often affectionately referred to as "opening exercises." Church school leaders in attendance at laboratory schools have observed that much more can be accomplished in a small class with a full-hour session than with either a thirty- or forty-minute session or a large-group assembly. Assemblies usually consist of hymns, prayers, Scripture reading, and announcements, many of which are also experienced in the church's morning service of worship. Why the duplication? In light of the little amount of time available and the real purpose of the Sunday church school, is such a large-group assembly really supportive of the church's ultimate objective? Many laboratory school students have returned to their churches to eliminate the departmental opening assembly.

Another area which merits examination is the relationship between a Sunday evening youth fellowship meeting and the evening service. Suffice it to say that it is frustrating when a good discussion must come to an untimely halt because someone insists that the young people be in the evening service. Adequate time is an important factor.

We have learned much in recent years about what is involved in the teaching-learning experience. Let us use these insights to help us shape the experience when youth and adults meet together.

## across-the-generations encounter

The teaching-learning experience should include an across-the-generations encounter. The advent and decline of youth movements and youth organizations in history is not accidental. It is related to the tension between youth and adults. Youth movements are generally associated with dissatisfaction and frustration over the ways adults think and act. They are a natural outgrowth of youth idealism and impatience. On the other hand, youth organizations can also be associated with the effort on the part of adults to be the leaders of youth: if not to direct them, then at least to influence them, to be their idols, and possibly even to control their thought patterns and actions. The youth organization has been described as the dissipation and adult takeover of the youth movement.

These arguments defend both the youth movement and the youth organization. The dissatisfaction of youth with things as they are is to be encouraged. And the desire on the part of adults to give guidance to youth and to contribute constructively to their character development is praiseworthy. Yet both groups and both motivations are guilty of serious shortcomings, among the most serious of them being that they are both seeking to take the easy way out (and here the youth organization is more guilty than the youth movement). Both are guilty in that it is easier for youth to ignore adults and for adults to pacify youth by seeing that they have an organization, than for the generations to have real encounter and dialogue with one another.

It is important that adults be challenged by the idealism, dissatisfaction, and daring of youth. For adults to fail to be exposed to these characteristics at a depth level is to deprive adults personally and corporately of something very significant. On the other hand, for youth not to be confronted by the perspective of history and realism which is more characteristic of adults is to deceive them about the world in which youth and adults must live together. Youth and adults must help each other to see that the sins of the world cannot be laid at the feet of one generation, and that neither generation by itself is capable of solving the world's problems.

This principle is leading many workers with youth to feel that legitimate and valuable learning comes from across-age-group experiences. Nothing quite takes the place of youth peer groups and relationships. Much is to be gained, however, when the generations meet to share.

One church is periodically forming groups of youth and adults for study and discussion purposes. Many denominational youth departments now conduct conferences in which the presence of adults in ratio to youth is highly intentional. Experience is supporting the belief that such youth-adult encounters are a more valid approach and a more honest coming-to-grips with the church's ministry with youth.

An illustration of the value of youth-adult dialogue took place at a Ministry with Youth Consultation. Four adults and three youth were discussing a movie they had viewed. One adult was saying that the film's drinking scenes, some social and some in excess, were realistic pictures of contemporary life but most unlike the day when he was a youth. He spoke of the time when social drinking was not at all common and when it had no place in the homes of churchgoing families.

One young person responded in amazement. He was dumbfounded to hear about a day when drinking was less common, and by the suggestion that there was something questionable about social drinking. Social drinking has always been with us, he said.

From the perspective of his brief, limited experience this young person was probably right; and it was helpful to the adults present to hear his words. They could not help gaining a better understanding of why many youth today are seemingly not troubled about drinking and often take a do-as-you-please approach to it. At the same time, it was good for the youth to hear the adults, for they could not help gaining an appreciation of why many adults in the church think as they do and express such deep concern over current trends in public behavior.

The teaching-learning experience will be strengthened by this kind of interchange. It often results in an encounter between youth and adults at a deeper-than-surface level.

What we are here suggesting, a meaningful youth-adult dialogue, is certainly against tradition, and, at least on the American scene, against culture. A. H. van den Heuvel, formerly of the World Council of Churches, develops the thesis that "youth work in a stable society is unnecessary." Accepting this thesis, our unstable society might therefore justify youth work. However, let us not fall into the error of using the terms "youth group" and "youth work" synonymously, and let us recognize the strong possibility that extreme consciousness of age-group grading leaves something to be desired.

## FOR DISCUSSION

1. Suppose we took seriously the sentence under the section on "Time": "Each church must find a pattern which enables it to be most faithful to its ministry with youth." What of our present program would we keep? What new patterns would we employ? Would we do any rescheduling? Is it worth trying to get objective answers to these questions?

2. Are our classes and fellowship groups too small or too large to allow for meaningful involvement? What can we do to improve the existing picture among our classes and fellowship groups?

3. There are both benefits and risks in exposing youth to adults and adults to youth. What might the benefits and risks be? Have student protests on college campuses come as a result of youth being exposed to adults too late or too soon?

4. Where and how might we begin an across-the-generations encounter in our ministry with youth?

"Adolescents Look at Family Clusters," in the Appendix, suggests another option in Christian education with youth.

# new relationships
# in new settings

DURING AN EVENING MEAL with two senior high girls the subject of conversation became the church of which they were members. Their least meaningful experience in church, they said, was the Sunday church school class. The teacher was not interesting, and the kids were bored. The lessons were dull and they dealt with things that seemed unimportant. As the girls described it, the whole situation was a mess, with the teacher receiving most of the blame. And, judging by what they said, one could not avoid agreeing that it was a mess.

The girls went on to describe their most meaningful experience. This was a Wednesday evening Bible study class, shared in by the same youth as those in the Sunday church school class. As my informants described it, it did not sound much like Bible study. However, they liked it because, as they put it, "We just sit and talk about what we want to talk about . . . the kids choose their own subjects . . . the leader lets us say anything we want . . . she's good."

As the girls compared the two experiences, it became apparent that it was the approach of the leaders that made the difference. I cited for them some reasons why they responded more favorably to the Wednesday evening Bible study than to the Sunday church school class. I pointed out the difference between the adult leader on Wednesday evening and the church school teacher on Sunday morning. I suggested that they approach their church's Board of Christian Education and ask for a Sunday church school teacher who was more like the Wednesday evening Bible study leader—only to have them respond, "Oh, it's the same person."

Aside from noting the unfortunate image this adult leader had of a Sunday church school class, let us observe that this negative response to a Sunday church school class is the reason why many youth drop out of church. These two girls will stay with the church, at least during their high school years, for they have the supportive ministry of parents. But what about young people who have no such support? And what of our ministry to those who have no relationship with the church?

## some new styles of ministry

One church follows the practice of recruiting Sunday church school teachers who commit themselves not only to Sunday morning, but to another meeting time with the class during the week. The midweek session is more unstructured than Sunday morning, with little or no concern about covering a certain amount of subject matter. It is more informal in character, something like the good experience cited by the two girls.

In the same community is a young adult who, supported by a nonchurch religious group, is seeking to minister to the non-church-related youth of the community. He spends much of his time at the community junior high and senior high schools, mingles with the youth in the school halls, is at the noon-hour dances, spends time on the athletic field and in the shower rooms, and frequents other places in the community where he can be with the youth. After establishing a relationship with a few, he invites them to a meeting. He makes the meeting attractive so that the youth want to meet again and again. Much of his time is spent in weekly meetings, which are usually held in the homes of persons interested in the purpose of the meeting. His ultimate concern is to "bring Jesus Christ" to youth who are not related to a church.

A working relationship has developed between this community youth minister and the staff of the church. When he feels that a young person is ready to be related to a church group, he directs him to the midweek session of one of the church school classes. This midweek meeting resembles more the kind of meeting the young person has been attending under the leadership of the community youth minister. The young people and the teachers of the church are ready to receive this young person. After he seems to feel at home in the midweek group he is encouraged to attend the Sunday morning church school session, the evening fellowship meetings, and the services of the church. The approach, therefore, begins with the less formal meeting with which the nonchurch-related youth can identify, and only gradually then is he related to some of the more formal church experiences.

Here is one pattern for relating to young people who do not and maybe will not gather at the church. It is a pattern which could become a part of the ministry with youth of more churches.

The situation we have described could be improved upon. Rather than being sponsored by a nonchurch religious group with financial support coming from outside the community, the community youth minister could be part of the staff of a local church, or a group of churches. Surely we can visualize a group of Baptist, Methodist, and Lutheran churches, for example, jointly calling a person and giving him the responsibility of relating to the community's church dropouts and nonchurch youth. This he may do on a personal and informal basis, through personal contacts with young people on high school and college campuses, or on a group basis, with the groups meeting on campus, in homes, storefronts, or other designated "halfway houses."

A group of twenty Protestant churches in one community are financially, and with personnel, underwriting a coffee house. These suburban churches, all near several college campuses, are making an attempt to have conversation with young people who for one reason or another are not voluntarily relating to the churches. Although established for the college community, the coffee house is also attracting high school young people. They now visit the coffee house in the evening between the hours of seven and ten, while the college students come later. Incidentally, in this same area a coffee house for adults has recently been opened.

Another pattern of ministry in which many churches are engaging is one beamed at public and parochial school dropouts and potential dropouts. Chances are that the school dropout is a church dropout much sooner. Thus, churches are making their buildings available and are providing personnel to work with children and youth who for one reason or another need help. Often, these young persons need help in understanding a subject they are studying at school. More often they are lacking in encouragement. The homes from which they come do not encourage excellence or the pursuit of knowledge, or are not conducive to study. A sizable percentage of the nation's school population is made up of "sitters," persons who are physically present but who do not participate in the social or academic life of the school. Concerning these youth, Dr. Gordon P. Liddle, associate professor of human development at the University of Chicago, says: "They lack a sense of identity with their teachers, with a majority of their classmates, and with school as an institution."

Among church members are retired school teachers, parents, grandparents, and college and high school youth who have qualifications for tutoring. In one church is a housewife who tutors a neighborhood high school girl in math. In another church, potential dropouts in the church's changing neighborhood are tutored by seminary, college, and high school students employed for that purpose. In many communities college students are volunteering to tutor youth—particularly black youth, who compose the majority of dropouts. Black youth who are out of school and who are also faced with the "last hired, first fired" principle challenge the church's faithfulness to the gospel.

Summer day-camping and resident camping offer the church

two of the finest instruments for relating to nonchurch youth. Most church camp-scholarship budgets are for church youth. If the money spent at the average camp snackery is any kind of guideline, most church youth do not need scholarships. Churches might well channel such resources into efforts to reach the unreached by giving to nonchurch young people some scholarship help for attending camp.

## a ministry geared to community needs

These examples and others illustrate how important it is for a church to turn to its community to discover how it is organized and then to organize its own ministry accordingly and appropriately. This kind of ministry necessitates a real knowledge of the community and its young people: the educational and employment patterns and opportunities provided for youth, their leisure time activities, their part in the community's crime rate, and other information concerning them. A special concern will be to discover the percentage of young people who have a meaningful relationship to the churches of the community, as compared to those who sustain no such relationship. Beyond this, the goal must be to implement the concern in such a way that it will result in a relevant ministry with youth.

One church failed to look at its community before moving out into a wider ministry with youth. The members decided that if their church had good recreational facilities and equipment, it would attract more youth. So they embarked on an ambitious building program and incorporated such facilities in their new building. They became disillusioned, however; for six months after the erection of the building there were no more youth than before. The church had failed to take many factors into consideration, not the least of which was the ultramodern high school only two blocks away, with recreational facilities and a program superior to what the church or all churches together could support. Why should they go to the church building?

Parenthetically, the church's concern for recreation was, in part, motivated by envy of another church which was receiving a wide response from youth to its dances. This particular church would not allow dancing, so it was struggling to find some other lure to which youth would respond.

Although recreation is a way of relating to many youth—and many more churches need to employ it in their ministry with youth—it is doubtful that recreation in itself will call forth, on the part of young people, the response to the ministry and message of the church that churches hope for. The primary response produced by recreation is recreation. This is a valid response, and the establishment of relationship justifies it. However, we will often need to be content to accept that response and that only, if recreation is the form of our ministry.

Having said this, we need to take a harder look at our attitude toward certain forms of recreation and do it from the standpoint of persons. Church youth are no different from other youth in that some have no difficulty making good use of their leisure time, while for others it becomes a time not for re-creation but for destroying property and persons. Some churches take a stand against dancing and successfully train their youth not to participate. Yet many of the youth who are trained in this way may instead spend long hours in dark cars "necking up a storm." Is your church getting ready for the era of more leisure time?

If we were to take seriously the community, the young persons in it, and the whole person—and if adults were to engage in conversation with youth at something other than the surface level—the church would not run away from the subject of sex. It is obvious that we do not get away from sex. The sexual revolution in which we continue to be engaged and to participate encourages premarital and extramarital sex and is surely making it much easier and safer. Contraceptives are something like seat belts; they reduce the injuries, but not the collisions.

To be sure, the percentage of youth who do not engage in promiscuous sexual relations is higher among church youth than that of nonchurch youth. We may take some comfort in this fact.

Hopefully, it will suggest another possible pattern of ministry with nonchurch youth. However, let us not forget that youth in the church do have problems. Their concern is not always the issue of sex, but whether or not someone will even consider them as a date!

## the stance for a decentralized ministry

What is your church doing to establish new relationships in new settings?

A certain stance needs to be taken by churches willing to undertake a decentralized ministry.

1. The community youth minister (or ministers), salaried or voluntary, will need to be relieved of responsibility for the gathered-church experience. He or she will have a relationship to all churches and will need to be fully aware of their structures and patterns of ministry. Insistence on this point will help to keep the community youth minister from falling into the bind in which most local church staff persons are caught: a time-consuming involvement in the gathered-church ministry.

2. The church will need to believe that what happens beyond the walls of the church building is important; that it, too, is "church work." It may not be couched in the vocabulary and patterns of the gathered-church experience. The approach may necessarily be different. However, more dramatic, life-changing experiences may also be taking place.

3. A church will need to understand, accept, and embrace this pattern of ministry as an evangelism which is based on God's love for people whether or not they come to the church building. One of the hard facts of the decentralized ministry is that all that the churches may gain from it is a sense of being faithful to their mission. The question always facing us is: How far are we willing to "go," or do we insist that they "come"?

What is more, the decentralized ministry will, of necessity, call for new approaches in leadership education. We have a fair degree of competency in helping and training the generally cooperative volunteer in the confines of the religious community. However, leadership education will now need to undergird the more "low key," freer, relaxed, one-to-one, small, personal group type of ministry. Leaders will need to be trained to work in unaccustomed fields, in cultures that are hostile; to be able to articulate the faith in territory where no one has an advantage and where the audience may not be a captive one; to be open to see and approach subjects from all points of view, and in all kinds of environments; to know how to deal with rejection and ridicule; to witness without being "churchy"; to speak God's word in our language.

What is more, churches will need to recruit leadership beyond teachers, counselors, scoutmasters. New categories may be introduced, such as walkers of the street, floaters for the hangout, friends for the gangs, mechanics for the car clubs, tutors for the dropouts. All of this is to suggest that the church does not conduct its ministry and recruit its leadership in isolation, but in close relationship and cooperation with other community agencies.

## FOR DISCUSSION

1. Does the immediate or larger community of which we are a part suggest and demand that our church engage in some type of decentralized ministry?

2. What special ministries are churches and agencies of the community currently engaged in? Are they doing any of these together?

3. What existing special ministries could our church immediately help to support? What are some new ministries our church ought to initiate?

4. Do the budget and activities of our church suggest that it is here to serve the community or to be served by it?

5. What will we need if we are to help our church membership understand the value and importance of such ministries even though they may not result in increased attendance?

"Notes on a Youth Ministry" and "Touch a Teenager!" in the Appendix, will stimulate discussion.

# among us leaders

THE CHURCH'S MINISTRY WITH YOUTH demands leadership—youth and adults who will give competent, creative, and constructive leadership—beginning now. Today will not permit yesterday's answers. A fast changing world exposes glib clichés. Faithfulness and mediocrity are incompatible. And to plan to begin tomorrow is irresponsible.

Leaders are achievers of answers. Followers are receivers of answers.

Followers are looking only for easy answers. Leaders know that there really are no easy answers.

Leaders know that the "how to" must be preceded by the "why?" Followers are prone to seek first the "how to" and then to ask the "why"—why it doesn't work.

Are you a follower? If so, it may be well to stop reading right now. For while the following paragraphs provide some answers to getting at a relevant ministry with youth, they are not easy one-two-three answers. The kind of answers here create work; they mean involvement; they may cause inconvenience; they require time, study, tension, some frustration, and a great deal of prayer.

But then, followers know something about all these—work,

time, frustration, tension. So what is the difference? Why not keep reading?

It is this way. There are answers which give solutions. And there are answers which give *direction* toward solutions. The latter is what the five following points seek to do—to give some direction to helping churches realize a relevant ministry with youth.

Leaders know that in the final analysis such answers are the only kind that can be given. Followers know this, also. So keep on reading, for in a real sense we are all leaders. Just remember, though, that none of us can "succeed in business without really trying."

## character and patterns of ministry

First, let us reaffirm (1) that the spirit of the gospel must characterize the church's ministry with youth; (2) that the conditions of congregation, community, and world determine patterns of ministry; and (3) that persons are the focal points of ministry. The mission of God is the redemption of the world. People are the object of God's love.

## engagement in mission

Second, let us remind ourselves that the purpose of the gathered-church experience is engagement in mission. The church is mission. Rather than draw attention to itself or think of itself as the great protector of the young from the community and the world, the church draws attention to God, to the community and world, and to what it means to live in them as the people of God. Thus, when the church is gathered, let it engage in experiences that enhance and give support to the witness of persons when they are dispersed. Let its projects implement the corporate involvement and ministry of the church in the affairs of the community and world in which the church is set down. The world in which we ask youth to live compels us to nurture them in the faith and in life itself so that, as the younger people of God, they may not fall and die to the world. For the sake of Christ they may stumble, fall, and die *in* the world, but hopefully not *to* it.

The time may come when it will be more important for Jane to attend the Pep Club meeting where a decision will be made on membership requirements than to attend a meeting at the church to plan the next three months' social activities for the youth fellowship; or for Bill to go to the specially called meeting at the Fraternity House to express his concern about the use of blackface in the proposed minstrel show than to attend choir rehearsal. Our purpose is not to encourage youth to give preference to church life over school life. Rather, we are to help them be faithful to the gospel in school life and in all other areas and relationships of life. The delegates at a youth conference in Asia said it this way: "Unless the present generation of Christian youth realizes the divine imperative in proclaiming the gospel relevantly, meaningfully, and powerfully to their contemporaries, the church will lose the very reason for its existence."

## organizing for mission

Third, whereas we earlier introduced the idea that "the era in which Christian education was done through youth organizations is largely over," let us not confuse a decline in "youth organizations" with the necessity for some organizing principle or pattern of organization for a ministry with youth. If an idea such as ministry with youth is to go beyond the idea stage, some kind of machinery, program, or method of attack must be put into operation. However, a pattern of organization based on the concept of ministry, and marked by flexibility and freedom and by a sense of purpose, is not so dependent on officers. There will be leaders, to be sure. But their leadership will be based not so much on position as on gifts and conditions.

What is more, let us not make the terms "youth organizations" and "youth groups" synonymous. Youth need and want youth group experiences, and a church may have many such groups as a part of its organized effort to minister with youth. However, it is not necessary that the groups be formally organized in the traditional sense, for example, with a president, vice-president, secretary, and treasurer. Several small, informal youth groups, not concerned for the maintenance of their own organization but rather motivated by an understanding of the church's mission, are a more valid way for a church to organize its ministry with youth. As a result they become therapy-directed (person-centered), study-directed (gospel- and world-concerned), and action-directed (involvement-oriented) groups.

## ministry with adults

Fourth, let us recognize the importance of the church's ministry with adults. Indeed, *a meaningful and significant ministry with youth rests on the church's ministry with adults.* Ross Snyder, a renowned youth ministry catalyst and writer, once asked a simple question: "Is there a future for the youth ministry?" He says that when he first went into full-time work in the church his feeling was:

If only I could get hold of the children and young people and kill off the parents and the adult church, I could do what had to be done. But, at the moment at least, I begin in the other direction. Unless the adult church commences to get a vitality and to some degree realizes the nature of the church in its operation, we are always being defeated in our work with children and youth. So that any of us who have primarily in mind a specialization in the church's ministry to youth must get in and pitch in the total program of the church, particularly in its relationship to the adults of the church.[1]

This statement suggests some possible consequences:

a. We will need to reevaluate our image of youth workers. The one who "has a way with young people" must also have a way with adults. A worker with youth must be as understanding of adults and as skilled in working and relating with them as he or she must be with youth. What is more, let us not be fooled by the old wives' tale that we need a young man to reach young people.

[1]"A Picture of the Minister to Youth," *The Chicago Theological Register,* 1956, p. 70. Used by permission.

b. We will need to rethink what we are requiring of a worker with youth. This is true of teachers and counselors in local churches, as well as of persons who have national and area responsibilities. Job analyses will need to put more emphasis on helping all adults (not simply those who work with youth) to become better persons and grow in their awareness of the world and of contemporary youth, with possibly less emphasis on "inspiring" youth.

For local church and area staffs, and, yes, national staffs, to fail to match leadership development opportunities for adults who work with youth with those provided for youth (admittedly a less dramatic and ego-satisfying venture) is something like standing at the base of Niagara Falls and shooting a water pistol. If area and national staffs have to make a choice about whether to work with youth or with local church workers with youth, let the latter be given priority. If a local church needs to choose between sending a young person and a worker with youth to a leadership conference, let it choose the latter. Pastors and directors of Christian education must come to grips with their own time and gifts. Are they workers with youth or workers with adults? Hopefully, they can be both. Realistically, one group must draw upon more of their specialized training. Let it then be the adult worker with youth. They who have the adults have the future.

c. The ministry which workers with youth have to adults will pick up at least the following concerns:

(1) Adults will need to assume their role as adults. Fred and Grace Heckinger, in their popularly written book, *Teen-Age Tyranny,* suggest that adults have abdicated their role. This thesis bears serious examination by adults, particularly parents.

(2) Before adults can speak constructively to youth about their attitudes, values, and behavior patterns, they will need to engage in serious self-examination, and, in words of Ross Snyder, "come clean" with the young.

(3) Adults will have to take seriously the words of Seward Hiltner of Princeton when he says that their ability to understand

and be relevant to "the real situation confronted by young people today depends upon dealing with the adult-adolescent relationship at something other than the surface level."[2]

(4) Adults, especially those involved in leadership positions, have little chance of becoming better persons and overcoming their personal insecurity and fear of youth without a serious biblical, theological, psychological, and sociological program of study.

## measuring results

Fifth, let us remember that youth's response is often difficult to measure, to recognize, and to focus upon. Of this we can be sure: The total response youth make to God's love in Jesus Christ will not be witnessed in the educational setting or gathered-church experience; the worker with youth may never hear or see the desired response; the desired response may never come; the response may not be consistent; the response may be very temporary; the response we do hear may be merely "the right thing to say."

In the final analysis, all we have to offer is our faithfulness to God's love in Jesus Christ. Unfaithfulness is our greatest problem. It is a tremendous deterrent to youth's response in faith and love. We do well to hear the real meaning behind the response of a Fair Housing executive. Answering the question as to what preparation the citizens of all-Caucasian Folcroft, a Philadelphia suburb, were given for the move-in of the non-Caucasian Baker family, he said, "Well, these people have been going to church for years."

## role of the Holy Spirit

Confessing that what we are really up against is ourselves, we also gratefully affirm that the Holy Spirit is at work in our ministry with youth. As D. T. Niles, the masterful writer of the book, *Upon the Earth,* says:

[2]"Adolescents and Adults," *Pastoral Psychology,* December, 1960. Used by permission of author.

The Holy Spirit is eliciting response in the hearts and minds of men to the working of God upon their lives. Their lives are lived within their faiths, sometimes as those who accept them and sometimes as those who do not. Into this situation, the Holy Spirit brings the witness of the Church to the Lordship and Saviorhood of Christ. This witness evokes the response of faith. It sometimes meets with rejection. It oftentimes results in raising questions in the minds of the hearers and leaving those questions there. The Holy Spirit takes all these ways in which people respond to the Gospel, and uses them in His own ministry of leading them to confess Jesus as Lord; or even where the confession is absent, of making Christ's Lordship a pressure felt upon their lives. The whole business is too complex for neat answers. We cannot meet a dynamic situation with rigid orthodoxies; we can only recognize it through lives of sensitive obedience. It cannot be otherwise since the mission of the Church is a mission within the mission of the Holy Spirit.[3]

## FOR DISCUSSION

The discussion, like the chapter itself, might seek to do some summarizing. Some questions for consideration might be:

1. What does "the spirit of the gospel" mean to you?

2. Give examples from history and the present scene of how the conditions of the community or the world have shaped ministry.

3. The phrase is used, "The church is mission." What does this mean? Is our church mission? Are we educating for mission?

4. What does it mean to be person-centered?

5. Is our ministry with adults adequate for a significant ministry with youth? Where is it strong? Where is it weak? What steps shall we take to equip adults better to work with youth?

"The Role of an Adult Leader," in the Appendix, will strengthen the discussion concerning "Ministry with Adults."

[3](New York: © McGraw-Hill Book Co., 1962), pp. 69, 70.

# appendix

## JOSEPH WILSON
# a letter to
# a potential christian
# disguised as a hood

DEAR BARRY:

For many hours I have pondered your remarks about not coming to the church any more. I must confess that I have to agree that it appears that there are people here that do not wish to have you around. Knowing these people, it seems to me that they fear you or fear what you might do to the church building or to their children. They do not know you as some of us do and their hearts have been hardened against loving you. You must understand, Barry, that they are good people who have worked hard for everything they have gotten. They have put a great deal of work into this church. They have been Christians in action as well as words many times in their lives. Because they have given so much, they do not want to see it destroyed or corrupted. Because of rumors and misunderstandings about you and your friends and primarily because you appear on the surface to be different from them, they fear to know you. This fear mushrooms; more and more rumors, true and untrue, along with exaggerations have caused them to follow through with the action that they have taken and no doubt will take in the future.

I realize that to you they appear to be the furthest thing from being Christians. I realize that what appears to be phoniness is all that you can see. I cannot bring myself to disagree with you on this. They are motivated by fear rather than by faith. I have a hunch that you are also. If your faith were real enough you would stick it through no matter what they thought of you, but then again where can you learn of faith if the church has no love for you?

Because you have changed so much, it is difficult at times for me to remember you as you were even a year ago. I can remember seeing you at a dance where you spent most of the evening in the smoking room. You were so unsure of yourself in the midst of others and so sensitive to every remark that came your way. You had a few friends then and you clung to those you had by not being chicken when trouble headed your way on a dare. I can remember how you defended your insecurity with the scoff and by picking on others with great cruelty. Those were the days when you never came around the church, because it stood for some mysterious authority that always seemed to be saying "Thou shalt not," and you knew that to exist in your society you had to live by the life-giving words of "You had better."

I remember the first night that you trusted me enough to go to fellowship. It must have been quite a shock to you as I look back. I know that it bored you no end. You left fellowship without giving it a chance, because you were sensitive to the silent glances of the members and the not-so-silent ridicule. I figured that we had lost you for good. But you came back, not to fellowship, but to my office during the week. Here you must have been a little more at home, because you kept coming back. I have often wondered why. Was it because of the freedom that you encountered? Was it because of the fact that I didn't say all the time that you couldn't smoke or swear? Was it because you were allowed to be yourself? Was it because I would clamp down on you when you lost control of your sense of humor? Or perhaps it may have been those quiet evenings when you would drift down just to sit and talk. How many things have we discussed? How many problems have we worked out together? How many times have you realized that you could let yourself go completely and even cry without being laughed at?

I remember the days when you came to the office just to sit in the background while the kids from fellowship took off their masks and entered into the many activities and lively conversations that always surrounded us. Happiness also surrounded this place. I guess you also recognized that they weren't all saints either. Perhaps this was the key. Perhaps it was there that you realized that you could be more than you were. I can remember how you first entered into the group. You found something in common with their sense of humor. You entered in easily because you didn't really have to prove yourself with daring feats. They were somewhat cold to you at first, but after a while you got used to each other. Do you remember the time Kenny or Wally first offered to drive you home? I guess it meant quite a bit to you, although you may not have shown it. Anyway it was easier to mix with them in the office after that and I guess it probably felt good when they said "hi" to you in the corridors at school.

I remember the Sunday evenings when you would come down to fellowship. At first you still could not get up enough courage to go to the meetings. You hung around outside smoking, or on the cold nights you stood inside. I can remember booting you out because I knew what would happen if other adults saw you loitering. But you always came back Sunday after Sunday. Then came the Sunday night when a couple of kids asked you to come with them to fellowship. You didn't really want to, but you went. You told me afterwards that you found it interesting, but your eyes told me that you still didn't feel at home. It took quite a while for you to come on your own. But it didn't really matter. You were always ready to help the kids run a dance to raise money, or to rake the lawns with them or to do all the other things that they did.

Do you remember the conversations that the kids had about God and Christ in my office or during the summer when you sat on the cemetery wall before you all decided to go swimming? I know for me these conversations were much more important than those held in Sunday school or fellowship, because they seemed more real and not put on. Each of these kids spoke his heart and I imagine raised a few questions in yours. I can remember the questions that you asked me when we were alone. They all centered in religious issues that you remembered from the early days when you went to Sunday school because your parents made you go.

Barry, I have watched your faith grow. I realize that you may not know all the books of the Bible, but you know what love is. You may not understand why God allowed Jesus to be killed, but you are concerned about other people. You may not understand why Catholics and Protestants are different, but you are able at times to pray. I have a hunch you know that God loves you just as you are, even though he hopes that you will become much more than you are. Barry, you belong in this church as much as anyone else. I know you find it difficult to explain that you don't want to come to church on Sunday morning because you don't own a suit coat. Sleeping late does have its advantages.

I have a dream, Barry. I have a dream that will carry the love of God and the fellowship of Jesus Christ beyond the doors of this building. I have experienced the meaning of the church many times in small groups meeting in many places—private homes and other places. The Holy Spirit works in other places besides the church buildings. God's temple is made of love, not stones or wood. I have a dream that will prove this, but I need your help to make it real. It is going to mean a lot of work on your part together with many other kids. We have a great responsibility, you and I, to make life worth living for the kids that are in the same predicament that you were a year ago.

Please take a chance and stick with us a while until we can make this dream come true. Perhaps then the adults of this church will be able to come together in a fellowship of love also. We have many miles to go, Barry. Let's go together.

In faith,

JOE

# WILLIAM W. FINLAW
## alec wants to know

ALEC IS A NICKNAME. My real name is W. Alexander Harrison, III.[1] Real impressive for a fifteen-year-old, huh? I'll bet you sort of picture me as an average, Caucasian, upper middle-class teenager, whose parents have plans for me becoming strictly upper class; thus the fancy moniker. But don't let the name fool you. I'm far from upper middle class, I'm far from Caucasian, and—I guess I gotta say it—I'm far from average.

Me, I'm strictly low, low class, socially speaking, and I'm strictly genius, intellectually speaking. How do you like that combination? But just because it is a rare combination, that's my claim to fame. What I mean is, I can see things from an entirely different perspective than the low-class, low I. Q. slum kid looking up sees them, and I can see things differently from the way the upper-class, high I.Q., suburban adult looking down sees them.

[1] W. Alexander Harrison, III, does not exist. And yet he does, in thousands of youth like him who have his problems and his despair, if not his insights into the difficulties Christianity has in reaching him. Alec is the creation of William W. Finlaw. In his work as Protestant chaplain to the Juvenile Court and related institutions in the City of St. Louis, Mr. Finlaw worked with many Alecs (and Alices) attempting to answer the very questions which Alec raises.

Don't you see how great this can be? Nobody in my situation is writing about my kind and our predicament. They haven't got the know-how. And nobody in the other situation can really do a good job of writing about me and mine, because they haven't got the know-what. So me—I aim to ask a few questions of the people who will be reading this, and, let's face it, the only ones who will be reading this are the "looking-downers." I aim to ask you a few questions that I hope will shake you up a little. Okay?

Before I ask these searching, penetrating questions—I used those two adjectives just to prove I am a genius—maybe you'd like to find out a bit more about W. Alexander Harrison, III, alias Alec.

I was born, out of wedlock, fifteen years ago last June in the charity ward of our city hospital. So you see, when people who have read this far are starting to think that I'm a sort of smart-aleck so-and-so, they're right on all three counts! Mama, she's worked on and off—mostly off—as a domestic (that's a glorified name for the kind of woman you call in when there's work that's too hard or too dirty for you to do), and she's okay; but she's had pretty much trouble with the men in her life. Brothers and sisters? Well, they're sort of related to her trouble, but if you really want to know, begin at the number fifteen and start counting down—you know—fourteen, thirteen, twelve, and so on, skip a number here and there (where kids have died, or Mama's been good for a while), and go on down to 1, and you'll get a rough idea of our ages and how many of us Mama is trying to support. My father? I never knew him. As I said, Mama had trouble with men, and every other brother and sister has a different last name; but I guess my father, W. Alexander Harrison, Jr., must have had pretty much on the ball, intellectually speaking, or else where did I get all my brains?

Home life? We have an apartment in a "de luxe" setting. Fifty years ago, I'll bet it was a real nice, single-family affair, but now we've got four families living in it, real cozy-like. We all share the same bathroom (when it's working), and I share a bed with two or three of Mama's other kids, and the whole family shares the same

9-by-11 living room, so like I said, it's real cozy. And in the winter we're glad it is cozy, 'cause that's about the only way we can keep warm!

There, I hope that little sketch will give you enough to go on as I begin to ask my questions. First of all, let's lay some ground rules, shall we? These questions are about you, dear reader, in relation to me, not in relation to my mother and her morals. Sure, it's easy to slough me off by pointing the finger of righteous indignation at Mama; but I'm asking these questions about me, the "innocent victim of my mother's folly." Hey, wouldn't that sound great with a violin playing in the background?

Okay, let's get going, shall we? Let's talk about things theological in this go-around. Let's talk about God and love, and Christian service, and Christian vocation and that sort of jazz. And remember, I'm only asking the questions. It's up to you to do the answering!

My preacher tells me that God created me. I'll buy that. He also tells me that God loves me. For the sake of argument, I'll even buy that. Finally, my preacher tells me that this God, who created me and loves me, also expects me to obey a few rules and regulations so that I can get to heaven one day. You know, honor my mother and father, no stealing, no coveting, and things like that.

So first of all, if I want to get to heaven, I'm supposed to honor sweet old Mom and dear old Dad. Come off it. When I look at her all I feel is disgust or pity. When I think of him all I feel is hate. So all I come up with is pretty dismal stuff. This God, who created me and loves me, put me into the situation I'm in, yet he expects me to honor two people who aren't worthy of the slightest bit of respect. If I honor them I'm a fake, so what I hear Christianity saying to me is, "Be a fake, if you want to get to heaven." Where am I wrong in my thinking? You tell me, huh?

Now let's look at stealing. Have I ever stolen anything? You bet I have! This God, who created me and loves me, put me into a family where there's no money at all for a so-called allowance. He has me at an age, and he's given me a color skin, where I can't find a job,

not even a crummy one. So what am I to do for life's necessities—
like candy bars and a soda and a movie and a dance now and then?
Well, the only answer I can come up with is to make like Robin
Hood. I swipe little things from the rich (who won't actually miss
them) to give to the poor, namely me. It's all petty larceny stuff;
I've taken shoes so I could go to school, clothes for the same
reason. I've grabbed a pair of swimming trunks so that I can go
swimming at a community center pool, and I've helped myself to a
little change here and there for spending money. Now, don't get up
on your high horse! I only steal what I've absolutely got to have, so
I can go to school, so I can get a school lunch twice a week (so that I
won't go hungry every day, at least). Yet the Good Book tells me,
"Thou shalt not." Okay, what am I to do? I humbly await your
suggestions.

   Last in this area, let's talk about coveting. Man, I spend every
waking hour doing just that! Maybe if I was like you and yours and
had a nice home and money to get even a few things, maybe then
I'd be satisfied and not have my mouth watering every time I pass a
restaurant or a clothing store. But I'm not like you, am I? So once
again I come up with a problem. Am I supposed to pretend I don't
want the things you take for granted? Do I have to be a phony, if I
want to follow the regulations of this God, who created me and
loves me? Isn't that what he is asking me to be—a phony? Okay,
"Dear Abby," what's the real scoop here?

   I've asked you three specific questions, but in my orderly and
logical mind, they are building up to an overall question which is
much more important. It is simply this: Doesn't God, and his love
and his regulations, actually fit you in your situation better than
they do me in mine? I mean, you probably had a mother and a
father who were worthy of honor. You probably never had to
steal. And you probably had enough of the finer things in life so
that your tongue wasn't hanging out for everything in sight. So
isn't Christianity more for you and your kind than for me and
mine? And don't you have to admit that you're asking me to be a
phony if I try to follow it? Answer me that to my satisfaction

(remembering that I'm smart enough not to be satisfied with pious platitudes), and you will really be doing all of us a big favor. But can you answer me? Friend, I don't think you can!

Every Christmas Eve, except one (and I'll explain that in a minute), one of our brood answers a knock on the door and is met by a fancy society matron bearing gifts; a few toys, some underwear and socks, a few canned goods and the like. She hustles in, breathing through her mouth so she won't get sick from the smells she isn't used to, and she says, "Merry Christmas from such-and-such a church." And we say, "Thank you" with much feeling and emotion, like this woman is heaven's gift to us (only we have to cram all that thanks into about ten seconds, 'cause it's obvious she wants to get out of there as fast as her fifty-five-dollar shoes will carry her), and she leaves. And the reason we say our thanks with so much emotion is because we learned our lesson a few years back. That's the year we didn't get any Christmas basket, and we found out later that the reason we didn't get one was because (and I quote), we "didn't act appreciative enough" the year before.

So once again I've gotta be a phony. I gotta pretend like you're the greatest thing on earth, so that you'll be willing to pretend that you're doing real Christian service in the years to come. Tell me truthfully, do you practice this charity once a year to meet my needs, or do you do it to meet yours, so you won't feel so guilty about what you're doing in relation to my real plight—like a decent place to live, like half a chance to be somebody someday?

I'll boil the main question on my mind down to this. Is Christian service giving me a Christmas basket, or a used coat you wouldn't be caught dead in (and added to this, I'd better act appreciative, or else nothing next year)? And if this is what Christian service is, me a phony and you a phony, do you actually expect me to get excited about it? Or to put it another way: Is Christian service, like God and love, something that works for you and your middle-class society; but isn't about to work for me and mine? Answers, please, I am waiting to hear!

Here I will quote (capitalizing on my terrific ability in such matters) from the same preacher who has been filling my head with these other ideas we've been talking about. "All work is God-ordained. Any job is a God-given vocation, and the dedicated Christian should see his work as a way of glorifying the God who created him." And do you know, if I were a doctor or a lawyer, or a businessman, or a skilled craftsman—in short, if I were middle-class and up, I think I could buy this. I expect you can. But close your eyes for a minute and conjure up an image. Watch me, standing on one end of a dishwasher in a big restaurant. There I am, sweating, chafing, hating this work reserved for winos and ex-cons and people like me. Now picture me shoving a big load into the machine, and saying loudly as I do, "Glory to God in the highest. Praise him from whom all blessings flow." How big a fake could I be? To me, the only blessing I can see is getting off from work, maybe with a bottle of wine to keep me company, so that I can forget that tomorrow it's gonna start all over again.

I've already made my pitch concerning this theological thought and its relation to the middle class, so I'll only ask you either to agree with me (in which case you can get off without explaining your answer), or to disagree with me; but then I want some reasons!

I've only scratched the surface of the questions I could ask you as we wax theological together. I sure could ask you a lot more. But maybe sometime, when other discussions come up and you're tempted to give quick and easy answers, you'll remember me. Maybe you'll stop and think, "Sure, that'll work for me, but how about Alec?"

I agree that you've got every right to be mad at me, humanly speaking. I am a smart-aleck so-and-so. But that's the way I am. And as I understand it, you're supposed to be concerned about me and my needs, no matter what kind of an impression I make on you. And believe it or not, I'm not asking you these questions to put you in a box. I'm asking you these questions 'cause I'd really like some answers, answers that won't make me a phony, answers that will *work* for me and my class like they seem to be working for you and yours. Will you try to help me? I sure would like you to, 'cause man, I sure don't see much sense to it all. And when you're brainy like me, things have naturally gotta make sense, don't they?

# JOSEPH WILSON
# notes on a
# youth ministry

LAST SUMMER IN THE CANADIAN WILDERNESS two teen-age boys taught important skills to a group of their peers on a difficult camping and canoeing trip. One excelled in campcraft and spurred the others into self-sufficiency. The other was a natural with the reflector oven and had the boys begging him to teach them his baking skill. The valuable leadership potential which came to life on this trip had, a month before, been channeled in the wrong direction. After many serious escapades these two boys had ended up in juvenile court for using a motor vehicle without authorization.

Before the trip they were rebellious teen-agers trying to be separated from a world they did not want. On the trip they expressed love and concern and tore away all the barriers which surrounded them. Oddly enough, the canoe trip held no magic within itself. This was simply the turning point for these boys—the turning point which was the climax of a ministry of love that began many months before in our youth fellowship.

After many frustrating and boring Sunday evening fellowship meetings, more or less dictated by the accepted type of youth activity that churches are supposed to carry on, the teen-agers de-

92

cided that some changes had to be made. The church was not meeting real needs nor was it using the potential within its fellowship. The ministry of Christ had been perverted into a social hour. Organization had taken the place of love, and ideas had taken the place of works.

Our teen-agers were faced every day with the problems of social relations, juvenile delinquency, lack of morality, indifference, and a shortage of jobs. If Christ could not enter into these situations, he could not be real to them. Something more practical than small-group discussions had to be found if the real meaning of Christianity was to be understood, accepted, and fulfilled by the teen-agers of our church. The protective walls that surrounded the church had to be broken down, and the church itself had to be taken into the reality of the world.

As an experiment, we set up our fellowship organization as that of a Gathered and a Scattered church. As a Scattered church, we became more concerned about other people. Adults in the church became interested in what we were doing and volunteered their services. We set up five task groups and each fellowship member was required to join one of them. Each task group met three times a month with an adult adviser to study a particular field or interest from a Christian viewpoint and to attempt to react as Christians. This meant not only understanding the problem, but also understanding our relation to it and perhaps more important, understanding ourselves and the reasons why we react the way we do.

A discussion evening was held with a Jewish youth group from a nearby town, sponsored by our Social Relations Task Group. The problems of minority groups and discrimination became a reality for those present. The teen-age Employment Task Group set up an employment agency, and in so doing became aware not only of the many management problems which arise, but also of the need to know and understand people better. Adult experience was recognized as valuable as teenage initiative. The task group on Juvenile Delinquency set out to understand these "creatures from another world" and discovered that they weren't really so different at all. The problems of cheating and of dating were taken up by our Task Group on School Morality. The Outsider Task Group sought to understand the withdrawn teen-ager and set about to catalog all the youth activities of the town and the requirements for participation. These were given to the town library to be put on file for any parents seeking information.

As these groups progressed, they began to realize more and more how secluded they had been from situations which they had taken for granted. Christianity could apply to all these situations, but only if they themselves as young people became good Christians. Their personal faith was weaker than they thought and they were now motivated to seek a stronger one.

As a Gathered Church, the task groups were responsible for one Sunday evening program for the entire fellowship, for the property of the church, and for the membership of the group. Worship under the leadership of a teen-age chaplain and his committee played a vital role in the membership. Meditations and Communion with the laying-on of hands by the minister became the most meaningful of experiences in the lives of these teen-agers.

Working together also became important, whether it meant serving on the Ways and Means Committee by raising money to cut costs on our retreats, or on the Properties Committee by painting, repairing, or cleaning sections of the church building. The Fellowship Committee set up a snack bar and recreation center for an hour each Sunday afternoon. This was open to grades six through twelve, since these were the grades that made up our three fellowships. Operating the recreation center involved buying, preparing, and selling food, and skill in leading recreation. As a Gathered Church, the fellowship grew stronger and nourished the work of the Scattered Church. Love became more important and teen-agers who had never bothered with the church before were now, at least, beginning to realize that such a place might hold something for them. New friends were made and trust began to develop. New interests were found and young people began to act on the assumption that the church might have something important to contribute to their lives.

The two boys who went on the canoe trip did not jump into these activities. Over the months they tested different areas of our church's life. Fellowship meetings themselves held little interest for them, but they helped on car washes and candy sales, and helped to clean sections of the church. On Sunday evenings they would mingle with the other teen-agers before and after the task group meetings. Slowly but surely they were making friends and beginning to understand what was going on. They even dared to attend our spring retreat.

Although most churches use retreats for program planning, we have placed our major emphasis on spiritual renewal, teaching, and work. On these retreats, which usually last from Friday evening to Sunday morning, we concentrate on a specific theme and attack it from all angles. We make use of prayer, literature, large and small discussion groups, meditation, movies, role playing, dramatics, panel discussions, etc. But the most interesting area, especially in gaining self-knowledge, is in our creative work. Here we make use of clay, wax, collages, coat hangers, pipe cleaners, creative writing in reaction to something said, written dialogues (perhaps between man and God), prayers, songs, etc. Through these media applied to a specific idea or topic, or at times to free thought, we confront ourselves, each other, and the Holy Spirit.

On one of our retreats, these two boys began to face themselves squarely and to recognize who they were. This was a very threatening affair for them. Since they were not ready for it at this time, they quickly replaced the barriers when the weekend was over. However, their contact with the church remained intact. They participated quite readily in the other very important aspect of our ministry.

During the week my office is a center for the teen-agers in the fellowship, and for teen-agers who have not worked their way far

enough out of their shells to become active in the fellowship. This
is the place where the delinquent and the high-honor college
student are treated with equal respect. The office is filled with
books and magazines, creative materials, chess and checker sets,
and a sense of humor. Anyone is accepted here, with the possible
exception of adults. It is here where most of the things that are
meaningful are born. The bluish-purple-and-orange decor reflects
the unusual role the office plays. It is a center for conversation,
a refuge, a problem-solving, problem-posing clinic, and a place to
seek for worthwhile individuals.

Needless to say, an atmosphere of freedom exists in which self-
discipline and control are necessary. Although this occasionally
poses problems for us, we will not change it because in this atmosphere of freedom the teen-agers get to know themselves and
each other as they can nowhere else. Hostilities are released and
healed, and Christ is experienced. Behind the scenes deep and
meaningful dialogue takes place among these young people who
are trying to know themselves and to make Christianity real in a
world that pretends it does not need love in order to function.

When our two canoe-trip boys were brought to court, the
church went with them. When they were placed on probation, the
church provided the friendship of teen-agers and the love and
guidance of adults to support them and to show them that they
were still accepted even if their deeds were not. The relationship
which began in the winter continued unchanged. In this atmosphere of love and freedom and creativity these boys were allowed
and motivated to mature at their own speed.

As a product of this atmosphere of freedom and creativity, the
teen-agers produced a paper called *The Agitator*. This paper is a
reflection of their own souls. It is a channel for creative writing
which seeks to show what they are feeling. In the past four years
the young people have dealt with such topics as "What Part of Me
Is Me?; "Christ Confronts the Teen-ager"; "Death"; "The Gentle
Place"; and a Christmas issue entitled "In Excelsis Deo and on
Earth Pieces." No formal publishing period is given, although the

members have attempted to release at least eight issues each year.

We are not yet satisfied with our youth ministry, but in this transition stage we are beginning to understand what Christ would have us do. Our philosophy is based on love as a motivating factor and we exist in a family atmosphere. Love comes through working and sharing together. Love plus confrontation with reality brings about redemption, which leads to personal commitment and mission. Our hopes and dreams and our work face toward the power of the apostolic church, on the one hand, and the people who are unprepared for today's world, on the other. Each church must work within this framework with its own potential. With the guidance of the Holy Spirit and the freedom to be committed Christians we will attempt to accomplish the daily tasks which are set before us.

## SHARON BALLENGER
# touch a teenager!

In the past few years behavioral people have concocted a large number of ideas for improving communication between parents and adolescents. The number of books, workshops, tapes, magazines, and movies on this topic is enough to boggle the mind. As a high school counselor, I come into contact with all kinds of problems, often with parents, primarily concerning some kind of communication trip-up. This next page or so will share with you some communication techniques and attitudes which I have found helpful.

Positive reinforcement, saying in some way "yes" to behavior and attitudes expressed, plus active involvement with the person talking can be valuable tools for parents to use in the home. A teenage girl who was in my office recently observed: "Mom talks mostly about the things I do that she doesn't like, or the things I don't do that she wishes I would." This is all too true for many of us parents. The ability to say "good" to a teenager at appropriate times will:

1. Give him/her positive feelings about himself/herself.
2. Cause the behavior to happen again.

Another skill I find helpful is one proposed by Dr. Thomas

Gordon in a book entitled *Parent Effectiveness Training.* He describes a unique way of learning to listen. In this process, the receiver tries to understand what the sender is feeling or the message means. Then the receiver puts his/her understanding in his/her own words and feeds it back to the sender—no opinions, no advice, no logic, but rather a statement of what he/she feels the sender's message means.

Active listening provides an open invitation for the teenager to talk. It requires a set of attitudes on the part of the parent or listener:

1. You must want to hear what is being said.
2. You must want to be helpful at this time.
3. You must genuinely be able to accept the feelings being expressed.
4. You must trust the teenager's or sender's capacity to handle the feelings, to work them through, and to find solutions.

Often it is difficult to just sit back and allow teenage problem solving to go on, free from our interference. A beautiful plus that comes from this special kind of listening, however, is that it enables us to influence our children. We influence them to make their *own* decisions. And that is a large part of parenting.

Another facet of communication, other than the exchange of words, is the nonverbal communication apparent in every interaction. When feelings cannot be freely expressed, nonverbal behavior often takes over. When I feel I cannot operate openly in a relationship, I physically withdraw to a safer distance. Looking directly at the person is extremely difficult. In long, boring, irrelevant meetings, I doodle a lot, cross my legs, my arms, look at the ceiling. My whole body shouts pretty loudly, "I don't want to be here!"

Body language often contradicts verbal communication. The young man in the psychiatrist's office assures the therapist that he really does love his wife, unconsciously shaking his head. Most of us, conditioned to hide our negative feelings, smile and respond pleasantly to other people regardless of the aches in the tummy and lumps in the throat. The head, because of all kinds of personal disasters in our lives, continues to throb as we smilingly greet the rest of the cast of characters in our world.

Another cultural hang-up which is destructive and inhibits communication is the lack of freedom we have to touch each other. Warmth, affection, closeness, and feelings of security happen when we are free to touch and be touched. A child who is cuddled and hugged has an excellent chance of growing up to be a loving, warm adult. The child who isn't, often grows up closed, shriveled, enveloped in a plastic box labeled "Don't Touch!" In the book *Peoplemaking,* Virginia Satir describes what happens to this kind of person.

> *If you keep too much of your inner space to yourself, barriers are quickly built up, which often lead to loneliness and a first step toward emotional divorce. Emotional divorces can exist* **between parents and children and between siblings as well as the married pair.** *. . . The taboo against touching and being touched goes a long way to explain sterile, unsatisfying, monstrous experiences many people have in their sexual lives. This taboo also does much to explain to me why the young person gets into so much premature sex. They feel the need for physical comforting and think the only proper avenue open to them is intercourse.*

The ability to "pick up" body language between family members, to experience your own nonverbal communication, and to touch your teenager often can cause more effective communication to happen.

I have found certain attitudes to be especially effective in my role as a counselor, wife, and mother. An important attitude is allowing the other person the freedom to be who he or she is. Attaching heavy expectations or neurotic personal needs to the people close to me brings communication to a grinding halt. When I can communicate to those around me that they really don't have to do anything to *earn* my love, that I care about them, that the ground rule in the relationship is not my expectations or their expectations but our expectations—the vibrations begin to be very good.

Let me admit to having difficulty with this seemingly "no strings attached" philosophy, ESPECIALLY with my children. I want my children to do well, I want them to be accepted in the real world, and I want them to be relatively stable earth-type creatures. However, I guess the observation I can make from my experience and from working with people is that most of us need to "cool it" and allow more freedom for growth and growing up in those we love—an attitude of trusting those around me enough to let go from time to time.

Realizing that the people close to me do not "see" life the very same way I do certainly enhances my ability to be with them in a more meaningful way. Each of us comes from a different background of experiencing. Our perceptions of what is real spin off from these experiences. Because none of us had the exact same bruises, itches, apple pies, and Band-Aids, we respond differently to bruises, itches, apple pies, and Band-Aids.

A person's behavior is strongly influenced by her or his perception of reality, which is based on his or her experiences.

In trying to understand how another person experiences life, I listen a lot and from time to time I say: "Let me see if I understand what you are experiencing right now with your boyfriend." There are times, because of my own frame of reference, I find that I haven't heard what is being said at all. A good rule to follow is: WHEN IN DOUBT, CHECK IT OUT!

A willingness to be open about my own feelings is an attitude I also find helpful in relationships. When I can share feelings, sometimes being gently confrontive when I'm puzzled or hurt, and give feedback when appropriate, I experience a deeper, more satisfying relationship with the person with whom I'm sharing. Instead of the Expert, the Supermom, or Suzy Homemaker, my family and friends experience a human being. The people in my life are also more able to be who they are as a result of my sharing. In this kind of communicating, TRUST becomes more than just a word.

I encourage you to move inside yourself. Look at your emotions. Then put your body and words together and share with a person close to you what you are feeling.

# THOMAS NIELSEN
# youth and the church

One day I was sitting in my office, looking at the pile of papers on my desk that had to be dealt with soon. The phone was ringing, there was a sermon to write for Sunday, a church school lesson to prepare, a Bible study to put together, and a counseling appointment that afternoon. I began to think as I reached for the phone—I am sure that you have had the same thought—"It sure would be nice to be in high school again. No problems, everything was so easy then."

After I hung up the phone, I began really to think about that wish. I began to recall the many agonies that were a part of my life then. I remembered the physical awkwardness, the "trauma" of wondering if I could get a date, the humiliation at having pimples on the night of that date. I also thought of the struggles I had with some questions of the Christian faith, of trying to test my own wings apart from my parents. I remembered talking with other kids about their troubles at home and with their families.

I began to wonder if life really was so simple. Did I really want to go through those problems again? Some of them from my perspective now seem rather insignificant, but then they were very important.

Then I remembered high school people that I have had contact with over the past few years, both inside and outside of the church. I began to reflect on the problems that they were facing and their cries of agony, the questions that they were raising: "Why can't I do anything right?"; "I'm so confused!"; "I'm pregnant, what do I do now?"; "Why do my folks fight all of the time?"; "Girls are sure funny. Why don't I understand them?"; "I don't know why I ran away, I just had to leave"; "Why won't the church listen to us?" As these questions went through my mind, I decided that I really wasn't all that interested in becoming a teenager again, not for anything.

What, then, does this say about the ministry of the church with youth? Merton P. Strommen in his book *Five Cries of Youth* lays out five of the significant areas of concern for teenagers today. They are the concerns of personhood, of family relationships, of social protest, of prejudice, and of joyous celebration. It is in helping the youth deal with these areas of his or her life that the church can have its most unique and powerful influence.

Let's look a little more closely at these areas of concern in the life of a teenager. The issue of self-identity is a crucial one. For on this hinges the self-confidence and self-reliance that all of us are searching for in our lives. The teenager is struggling with this issue on many fronts. The issue of identity apart from one's parents heads the list. The young person has to develop the sense of self-worth needed to rely on his or her own resources and not on someone else's. The teenager is moving to discover his or her own set of skills and interests and is unsure of the degree of skill that is possessed. As one begins to date and mix socially, again issues of identity and self-worth spring up.

The matter of family relationships is of concern also. Family conflict, unwillingness or inability to deal with certain issues, divorce, and insecurity about one's position in the family add up to some real tensions in the life of youth today.

The concerns of social injustice and prejudice are certainly a part of the youth culture. The question of "Why is the world like this?" is part of the makeup of youth today. Youth in general are more tolerant of differences and are more willing to become involved in an issue than was the case one or two decades ago. They have great concerns about many situations and are impatient for change. However, the intensity of these concerns seems to be declining somewhat.

Finally the matter of joyous celebration is part of the life-style of youth. Celebrating in an open and joyous manner is truly a part of their way of doing things. A chance to celebrate the successes of life is definitely a part of what they are looking for as a major concern of their lives.

The church has a unique opportunity to minister to youth in these five areas of concern. Responding to the needs and cries of youth is the ministry that the church can have if it is willing. There are few, if any, other places in our society where teenagers, or anyone else for that matter, can really deal openly and honestly with all of the concerns of life. For in the church there is the potential of bringing together all of the influences that go into a whole person, the "secular" and the "spiritual." The potential is great. Are we willing to strive to reach it?

The question that each church must face is whether or not it is willing to pay the price for this unique ministry to be a reality. There are risks involved. Changes in the way things have always been done may have to occur. Some priorities may have to be shifted in order to fund adequately a ministry with youth that confronts these life issues.

In the church, a setting where love and acceptance are the standard of relating to each other, the hard questions can be asked. In the Christian fellowship the "hows" and "whys" of the world can be explored and some answers found. The community of believers provides the celebration in times of joy and the support in times of pain and crises. This can be the potential for the church.

In fact, this is the type of church that youth are seeking in their quest for meaning in life. There is a desire to be a part of a fellowship of believers; but there may also be a real misunderstanding of, if not disdain for, organization and institution. This causes great concern and worry among those who work in local church youth groups and among church parents. In their search for a supportive fellowship of people, youth may reject the church that they have gone to since being in the nursery. Immediately we feel that they have rejected the Christian faith. Parents begin to use many different tactics to get their child back into the worship service of their church. What we often fail to recognize is that in most cases, the teenager may be rejecting not so much the Christian faith as he or she is rejecting the institutional church.

Youth seem to have generally made the distinction between the "church" as organization and "church" as a community of believers. This, coupled with the need to develop one's own faith independent of influence of parents, leads to a rejection of the organized church. The conflict arises because it is this very organization in which we are able to work and search for an expression of our faith and Christian community. The institutional church of today can still meet the needs of youth. It is doing so now for many youth in many communities. But in many others it may have to change to be able to minister adequately. An interesting point is that while youth within the church make the distinction between the "church" as people and the "church" as building, those outside do not. This then makes ministry to these two groups distinctly different.

Youth have varying commitments to the church as an institution. These commitments tie in directly to the ability of the church to meet the needs of their lives. For some the commitment is great and for some there is none at all. Our challenge is ever to increase our abilities to make our churches fulfill the potential that is present. We must seek to be the type of community that can respond in an authentic manner to the cries of youth. And we must also be a community that raises the challenge of ministry as well.

When an individual church makes an assessment of the needs in the lives of the youth of its community and compares that with the opportunities available for ministry, then it can begin responding in the unique way of which the church is capable. The church does have a unique ministry. The youth of our churches and the youth who have rejected the institutional church are searching for that very uniqueness. They are searching for a group of people that will accept them with their questions and their problems and their ways of celebrating. They are searching for relationships in which they are free to be themselves so that they may discover themselves. That is where we are called to minister as we expand our ministries with youth.

# leader profiles

## authoritarian

One of the leaders, Mr. Arthur, is outstandingly *authoritarian*. Before his class of senior students he stands with Bible and quarterly on lectern. He has a simplicity about him that is appealing and also a kind of assurance.

He begins the study with a well-rounded overview of what's coming, then launches into exposition of the Scriptures. Questions follow that have obvious answers, and sometimes Mr. Arthur moves quickly to answer them himself, especially if class members hesitate and break the flow of the study that is going along nicely. No one has ever known Mr. Arthur not to know the answer to a question, and nobody ever has to do any thinking on his own. Mr. Arthur does that for him.

Funny thing, Mr. Arthur sure has *his* authorities. To his credit, he claims God as his highest authority and wants to take his cues from him. Among mortals, there is a former pastor, the writer of the curriculum material, the church, a teacher he had when he was younger, a politician, and a parent. He refers to what "they" say, meaning one of the sources of his authority.

If one of Mr. Arthur's questions is answered in a surprising way or is at variance with his viewpoint, the class knows what Mr. Arthur is about to do: Set things straight! If the discussion "gets out of hand," Mr. Arthur may hold the class overtime. He is fearful of not having explained everything or "gotten everything across."

Mr. Arthur hears talk about the needs of young people, but he doesn't worry about that. He believes the truth in the Word is in balanced enough form that taking it "like it is" and presenting it week after week without discovering its specific relationship to youth needs will get the job done.

The class members are pretty well disciplined. Sometimes threats have to be made. But most people understandably like Mr. Arthur because he is a sincere man. Many look up to him and say he really knows what he's talking about.

When you leave his class you have a good, settled feeling, like, "Well, that's been taken care of!" The class hasn't been disturbing, like a lot of things you read now.

Sometimes the students grow frustrated, however, and feel as if they've been treated as though they were a lot younger than they are. Nobody wants to hurt Mr. Arthur's feelings and disagree with him. He goes on and on just as he always has.

## laissez-faire

The freshman class has an attractive, middle-aged teacher, Mrs. LaFever. Possibly she could be classified as laissez-faire in her approach to church school leadership. She deliberately refuses to give direction to the class members.

Mrs. LaFever works long hours at her job, is usually tired, and does not enjoy preparing for her work as teacher of sophomore youth. She has read a couple of books on unstructured group work and once attended a lay retreat where she felt she benefited from group dynamics. She feels disillusioned about her own strict upbringing and wants no part of the tactics that her parents and teachers used, which now seem manipulative to her.

Mrs. LaFever goes to her class some Sundays with a poem and a verse of Scripture, which she hopes she will not have to contribute. The class will probably talk about parties, exam week, and the coming holidays. The study is from the Old Testament and seems so remote.

The class will talk and giggle and pass around pictures on one Sunday. On another Sunday, everyone will be strangely quiet. Mrs. LaFever likes for them to talk, for then she feels thay are expressing themselves and "getting something out of it." Occasionally a youth does bring up something that is really important. Then the group shares the concern, offers advice, and perhaps throws light on it by remembering verses of Scripture that are applicable.

Sometimes the class takes turns reading verses of Scripture from the quarterly and commenting on them.

The youth brag to their parents that the teacher allows them to take the responsibility for the class; to set the standards of behavior; to determine what, when, and how to go about the study. They feel that Mrs. LaFever tries to be one of them. They say that she says she understands them. She even remembers a church school class from her younger years where they just talked about ball games and things.

Mrs. LaFever likes the class, feels they have good ideas, and will have them over to her house soon for a cookout.

## democratic

Mr. Demarco is director of the church school High School Department. He's a really live man, always listening, trying out ideas on people, taking people seriously. You might call him a *democratic leader.* I know I would.

Mr. Demarco is always prepared, but usually not for a lecture. He has talked with his young people about their expectations and needs for this quarter—has mulled over what they said. Together, they are coming up with discussions, panels, skits, speeches. Mr. Demarco advises, encourages, scrutinizes, criticizes, urges on, and holds back. There are moments when he is silent. Mr. Demarco, like Mr. Arthur, believes the Bible is true, but he feels that interpretation of the Bible can be questioned.

Mr. Demarco is a participant. He may lecture at times. The proof of his style comes when his lecture is finished, for then he listens, responds, and listens again. He does not act miffed if someone takes issue with the very heart of what he has laboriously prepared. If there is not enough time for adequate response following his lecture, he may phone several youth after church. He knows the members of his department better than other leaders do, because they have shared themselves with him.

Mr. Demarco aims for insight and behavior change. He is vitally interested in helping young people cope with life problems. He knows he cannot give them ready-made solutions for all of the novel situations they will meet in the future.

Mr. Demarco continuously applies critical standards to what he is trying to do. Are the members gaining in a knowledge of Bible material? Are they involved in solving problems that they face? Are they increasing in their capacity to care about others?

Sometimes the pastor takes note of the group spirit in this particular department. Something is going on within this group that is producing real fellowship.

The young people are not always comforted by this part of Sunday morning. Sometimes people tell Mr. Demarco that they wish he had more answers and fewer questions.

## your style of leadership

The following is a test that may prove helpful in identifying your usual way of relating to your church school group. Circle the "yes" or "no" beside each question.

Yes No  1. Do you seek to get some response from every member of the group?

Yes No  2. Do you consider it unimportant to orient your group to the content of a unit?

Yes No  3. Do you often lecture?

Yes No    **4.** Do you lack specific goals in your church school work?

Yes No    **5.** Do your approaches and methods of Bible study vary from Sunday to Sunday?

Yes No    **6.** Do you recognize the value in sharing different viewpoints?

Yes No    **7.** Do you feel little concern about the result of the session?

Yes No    **8.** Do you often find yourself pretty upset when others do not agree with you?

Yes No    **9.** Do you go into sessions with little or nothing planned?

Yes No    **10.** Do most of the people in your group relate to you as if they feel inferior in their knowledge and understanding and hesitate to "be themselves" when they are in your presence?

Yes No    **11.** Is your group relaxed but under control, verbal but not noisy?

Yes No    **12.** Do you think that you must always cover all the material?

Yes No    **13.** Do you usually not know what will be happening in your group fifteen minutes later?

Yes No    **14.** Do you do most of the talking?

Yes No    **15.** Are your youth increasingly making decisions on the basis of their own beliefs?

Yes No    **16.** Do you feel completely responsible for the outcome of the study?

Yes No    **17.** Has it been a long while since your group had a session that seemed to zero in on *important* issues?

Yes No    **18.** Do you often work with your group in the planning of future activities?

Yes No    **19.** When you ask a question, do you usually have only one answer in mind that can be correct?

Yes No    **20.** Do you feel quite comfortable when views

that you consider undesirable or downright false
are presented?

**Yes No** **21.** Have you in recent months seen something in
a different light because of insights that were
shared during the Bible study session?

## now evaluate:

If your answers were "Yes" to numbers 3, 8, 10, 12, 14, 16, and
19, you may tend toward an authoritarian approach.

If your answers were "Yes" to numbers 1, 5, 6, 11, 15, 18, and 21,
you are probably pretty democratic.

If your answers were "Yes" to numbers 2, 4, 7, 9, 13, 17, and 20,
you are perhaps more laissez-faire.

By now, my biases are showing! In all fairness, however, let's say
that a warm, interesting, informed, good authoritarian leader is
probably better than a leader who tries to use democratic methods
but is lacking in kindness, patience, and knowledge. Personal
offensiveness is quite aside from any particular method! A case
could certainly also be made for a permissive approach, *if* the
leader is trained to lead in unstructured situations.

Experiments to determine the relative subject-matter achieve-
ment of authoritarian and democratic approaches are inconclu-
sive[1] and ". . . some manipulation is necessary to arrange the
learning situation and to bring the learner face to face with
stimulating problems."[2]

Studies do seem to show that democratic methods of leading
tend to foster "enthusiasm, spontaneity, work initiative, coopera-
tiveness, mutual respect and friendliness."[3] Most people who try
it, like it.

[1]Herbert Sorenson, *Psychology in Education,* 4th ed. (New York: McGraw-Hill
Book Co., 1964), p. 493.
[2]Henry Clay Lindgren, *Educational Psychology in the Classroom,* 3rd ed. (New
York: John Wiley & Sons, Inc., 1967), p. 326.
[3]Sorenson, *op. cit.,* p. 495.

# MARGARET M. SAWIN
## adolescents look at family clusters

What have youth been saying about family clusters — "the church education program with families at its center"?

"My cluster helped me to relate to other adults and to get to know other parents."

"Our cluster is the one thing in a week which draws our family together."

"I noticed that studying about conflict in the family helped me in my family."

"Religion deals with life, and cluster deals with life."

### what is a family weekly cluster?

These were some of the comments a number of our youth expressed in reaction to being a part of a family cluster this year. The family cluster is a gathering of five or six families. They support each other and are part of an educational experience in which every family member is a full participant.

**114**

## family cluster goals

1. To provide an intergenerational group of families where children and youth can easily relate to adults, and adults to children and youth.
2. To provide a group which supports and respects its members.
3. To help parents better understand their children through contact with other children, and, likewise, to help children to gain a better insight into their parents through contact with other parents.
4. To provide an opportunity for families to work on issues and topics related to their faith, to themselves as individuals, and to their family life.
5. To provide an opportunity for families to model and share their own family's style of decision making, disciplining, interrelating, problem solving, etc.
6. To provide an experience where adults share their concerns regarding the meaning of life's experiences amidst a time of rapid social change and aberration of traditional values, and where youth can deal existentially with their real world experiences and check them out in a supporting group of other youth and adults.

## experience teaching

To further these goals, a model of experiential education is used. Members of the cluster have an experience together and then discuss the experience. Experiences include: simulation games, role playing, finger painting, clay modeling, storytelling, creative writing, collage making. With this approach, young children can participate and learn from an emotional response, while other children and adults can participate and learn from a cognitive response.

## family contract

Children and teenagers agree to a family contract whereby each member of the family contracts to be in a cluster for a certain number of weeks. The cluster contract of the families as a group also assures that teenagers, as well as children, have a voice in cluster affairs and are heard. They know that they are an important part of the group and they respond to the group in a responsible way.

We interviewed fifteen youth as to their feelings about being in a cluster and the kinds of experiences they saw as valuable through membership in such a group. The age spread of adolescents was one twelve-year-old, six thirteen-year-olds, one fourteen-year-old, three fifteen-year-olds, and four sixteen-year-olds. The interviewed group was composed of six girls and nine boys. Most of the adolescents had been in a cluster two years. One of the healthy points of cluster is that all children and youth like to be present and enjoy the general format. They form an intergenerational peer group together that can play, joke, and interact with each other.

## youth and adult friends

Adolescents felt that one of the greatest assets the cluster experience brought was helping them to become sincere friends with numerous adults, and to be taken seriously by them. In our culture there are few places where adolescents meet a number of adults, other than their parents, and act with them for lengthy periods of time. Almost all the teenagers said that when they see a "cluster adult friend" at other functions within the church setting, they don't panic and think, "What am I going to say to this adult?" Rather they consider the adult as another friend with whom they can easily share things in common. To accomplish this, we often divide into pairs or triads within the cluster, allowing for a cross-generational "mix." Another activity is using "simulated families" where the father of one family, mother from a second family, and children from a third are brought together in a "pretend family." This may occur when we are discussing a topic too threatening to handle within their own family setting, or the simulated family may make up a role play to present or do some other activity together.

## the whole family together

Family cluster is one setting where the whole family is together for a learning experience. Many youth indicated that it is often the only activity in which the family participates together during the week. Most church programs are based on the "split-level approach." Children go to one classroom, teenagers to another, and adults someplace else. We believe that parents are the primary teachers of values to their children who, in turn, learn to refine their values by discussing them with other persons. The teenagers also felt that discussion in cluster helped them to understand adult thinking and allowed the opportunity to question and discuss adult ideas and comments. If the church does not provide for adult-youth conversations, we are neglecting an important part of value education for adolescents and adults.

## we came to like our parents . . .

Teenagers also felt that clusters provide an opportunity for them to see how unique their parents really are. It helped them better understand and thereby allow for more tolerance of their parents' personalities and values. The cluster experience helps a family look at itself and perhaps understand facets of its own functioning which may never have been articulated or pointed out. It helps to dispel family myths. It allows both youth and parents to understand the reality of family life and the role of parents. Teenagers are exposed to the realism of parenthood through people other than their own parents. Parents see themselves through the eyes of other youth.

## stronger families

Family clusters also provide an avenue in which families can watch how other families operate, function, and live out their concerns. A family can see how another family interacts and then consider change in their own living because of this new awareness. Such an experience permits teenagers to enlarge their vision about modes of family functioning. It gives them other alternatives to consider in their styles of family living.

Multiple-family-therapy research shows that families help each other to change and grow more than the therapist does. Therefore, we assume that families also help each other by being together in a family cluster. Our adolescents seem to think this was true. The act of discussing uniqueness, differences, and their feelings themselves helped them feel closer to each other as family members. *This meets one assumption of the Family Cluster Model: that, in stressing diversity, we often promote more acceptance and thereby closeness and affection among family members.* At a time of lostness, aloneness, and confusion in our society, it is good to have adolescents feeling that their family ties are becoming stronger.

## cluster curriculum

The specific context of a cluster is developed at the request of families. Possible directions include:
—communication within the family
—authority and power in the family
—conflict and its resolution
—beliefs and values
—our sexuality and its importance
—what about grief and death?
—transactional analysis of our interactions
    (based on Eric Berne's theory)
Several teenagers, in our interview, mentioned that the unit on conflict/resolution changed the way they related to other family members. The unit on beliefs helped them to articulate better what they believed in. A number of them felt that cluster taught them about the importance of personal relationships and, therefore, life in its larger scope. One said: "Religion deals with life, and cluster deals with life in an up-to-date way—so our beliefs and actions often come out of cluster." (To me, this is religious nurturing at its best.) At the same time, however, some adolescents were not aware that cluster learning is religious. They defined "religion," as

"something to do with worship in church." They were unable to interpret religion into everyday life. Therefore, unless we can help persons associate their interpretation of religious meanings with their day-to-day behavior, we become "sounding brass or a clanging cymbal." **Religion is a force by which one lives**—not a ritual undertaken once a week. Children and adults need to be exposed to religious ideas daily through their family living. Cluster can serve as a place where this is emphasized.

## cluster education is fun

One aspect of cluster which the youth emphasized was that of having fun. Cluster is a place where they meet friends of all ages, play games, participate in sports activities, and have fun during the meal. They said, "We know there is a fun side to religion; we don't just read the Bible!" They especially liked an all-day planning retreat in the fall and a concluding weekend retreat in the spring. They disliked "stupid" experiences which made no sense to them and also evaluations at the conclusion of study units. **They would have liked the cluster period of two hours per week to have been longer!**

One of the healthy aspects of cluster experience is the family "spin-offs" which happen as a result of having been together. Often a discussion is started in cluster which is continued in the car driving home or later at home. At that time, parents become the "interpreters" to the youth of what has been happening with cluster. This encourages the parent to assume his rightful place in the religious nurturing process of his child. The Jewish home has kept this process within the family. This has been one of the reasons why the Jewish people have been able to maintain a strong faith identity. When we "loan" out our children to the church school, we are encouraging parents to lose their right as interpreters of the faith. Parents and churches need to work more diligently at helping the process of "family building" within an age of pluralism and mass media.

# GARY BARMORE
# the role of
# an adult leader
# of youth

## "what am I supposed to do, anyway?"

This cry, often heard from adults tapped for youth ministry leadership in the local church, means we need a proper understanding of the adult roles involved in this ministry. The definition of roles that significant adults can play in their relationships with youth is the purpose of this article.

While affirming the tenet that "youth are the church *today* as well as tomorrow," this article assumes that *adults do* play a valid role in shaping and effecting a church's ministry with youth. And while affirming the conviction that "youth ministry is the responsibility of the whole congregation," this article assumes that a few *specific* adults will fulfill definite responsibilities as youth ministry leaders.

## "so what are you going to do about it?"

The first task is to seek general guidance from two sources: (1) contemporary explorations into adolescent identity development and healthy youth-adult interactions; and (2) our biblical/ theological heritage which offers foundational principles for church life. Then, the second task is to suggest specific role categories through which adults can best relate to youth in a local church setting.

## "what do the pros say?"

(contemporary explorations into adolescent identity development and healthy youth-adult interaction)

Erik Erikson, professor of human development at Harvard, calls the central problem of adolescence "identity confusion," such as articulated by Biff in Arthur Miller's *Death of a Salesman:*

> *"I just can't take hold, Mom, I can't take hold of some kind of life."*

The confusion increases when the young person also faces doubt concerning ethnic or sexual identity or cannot settle on an occupational direction.[1]

The maturing process is best facilitated when the adolescent can discover persons and ideas "to have faith in" (a trust which he can even test through blatant cynicism). IDENTITY BLOSSOMS IN IDEOLOGY. Facelessness evaporates in faith (of some kind). The chief role of existing institutions is presenting youth with ideals which adults and youth can both share and which, in Erikson's words, "emphasize autonomy in the form of independence and initiative in the form of *constructive work.*"[2]

Erikson's framework also includes the process of intimacy development. These "psychosocial intimacies" may take the form of friendship, dating, or group inspiration.

This combination of constructive work and intimacy parallels William Glasser's contemporary dictum concerning every person's two basic needs: (1) to love and be loved, and (2) to feel worthwhile.[3]

Sociologists would stress the dynamics of the group in the

[1]Erik H. Erikson, *Identity: Youth and Crisis* (New York: W. W. Norton & Company, Inc., 1968), p. 131.

[2]*Ibid.*, p. 133.

[3]William Glasser, *Reality Therapy* (New York: Harper & Row, Publishers, 1965), p. 9.

process of identity development. Although an adolescent finds himself in many "membership" groups (e.g., race, neighborhood, family, school, church, clubs, teams), one group usually serves as a "reference" group. From the reference group, he derives the values, norms, and attitudes which provide his chief identity and which inform the manner in which he chooses and relates to the various membership groups.

## "let's get the Bible into this!"
(our biblical/theological heritage which offers foundational principles for church life)

The Bible points to the same insights as contemporary psychology and sociology. Loving and being loved is the chief attribute of the Christian community (John 13:34-35), and God's people are to be about the worthwhile labor of their Father's business (Genesis 1:28; Matthew 25:40; 2 Corinthians 6:1). In conjunction with the *individual* development of purpose, the Bible also describes the crucial function of *group* dynamics. Scripture indicates that although God relates his love and salvation to individuals, the context out of which Christian living proceeds— the matrix within which nurture occurs—is a COMMUNITY of believers (1 Peter 2:9-10).

In the fourth chapter of Ephesians, the apostle Paul offers counsel for the life of this community. The insights are appropriate to the current youth ministry scene. In verses 12 and 13 Paul sets forth two basic *goals* for a youth group:

... *building up the body of Christ* ...

... *mature manhood* ...

Toward these goals of healthy group/church life and maturing personhood, Paul suggests two primary **methodologies:**

**MUTUAL MINISTRY,** in which all are ministers and some have a focused role of preparing and enabling others to fulfill their own unique gifts of faith and action (verses 11 and 12— some pastors/teachers for the equipment of the saints for the work of the ministry . . .).

CARE-FRONTING, wherein relationships of love strive for a balance of honesty and tenderness (verses 25 and 32—"putting away falsehood, let everyone speak the truth with his neighbor . . . and be kind to one another, tenderhearted, forgiving one another . . .").

## "you still haven't told me what to do!"

In light of this background of theology and social science, the role of the adult involved in youth ministry begins to take shape. The many dimensions of this role fit into three basic categories.

*Model: one whose attitudes and behaviors offer a pattern which can be considered by others for adoption and adaptation.*

MODEL—The adult who works with youth can offer a visible demonstration of both *competency* and *vulnerability*. That is, the adult provides an example of a growing human being who possesses adequate skills for life and faith, yet can admit to problems, fears, wounds, and wrongs. The adolescent, seeing such behavior and attitude in a significant adult figure, can then "try on for size" actions which manifest his abilities or reveal his deficiencies. Observing adults who handle both of these with growing maturity increases the probability that youth will develop healthy ways of balancing their ideals with a fairly accurate perception of reality.

Modeling also provides the primary vehicle through which youth embrace Christian faith. No matter what materials, techniques, and programs are used, the factor of personal faith is present in the adult model. Most Christian adults grant that the key ingredient in their commitment to Christ when they were young came *via* the influence (usually life-style, not words) of a significant adult.

*Enabler: one who makes another able, who offers means toward adequate skills and knowledge.*

ENABLER—The enabling dimension is generally more active than modeling. Here the adult functions as a teacher and imparter of skills; the styles of instruction can range from lecture to group discovery.

Enabling youth ministry also means the exercise of loving and just authority (not authoritarian*ism*) by the adult wherin he has been delegated responsibility according to the laws of the state or the guidelines of the church. Maintaining discipline (and remember, the word is related to "disciple") not only safeguards the health of an individual adolescent but also can help ensure an atmosphere of responsible freedom in which the liberty of one does not jeopardize the well-being and freedom of others.

Sometimes the enabling role includes a strongly confrontative character, but only where a relationship of trust and care is being fostered. The adult can be a reality factor to enable the idealism of youth to find rewarding (more than thwarting) channels of work and to enable the intimacy experiences of youth to find satisfying (more than frustrating) channels of companionship.

*Friend: a person attached to another by feelings of affection or personal regard.*

FRIEND—Although the previous two dimensions include elements of friendship, the specific role of adult-youth companionship must be stressed. Despite occasional protests to the contrary, youth desire close contact with adults.

Obviously this doesn't mean the adult becomes a "kid," for then it no longer is an *adult*-youth relationship. But it does mean the adult takes time to hear, understand, and perhaps even enjoy the world of youth. It means the investment of time, emotion, and energy. It means a healthy self-respect by the adult, so he need neither be overwhelmed by nor dominate the young person.

The "adult friend" role can complement or confuse the young person's relationship with his parents. Youth can share with adult leaders concerns they are unable (through embarrassment, rejection, privacy, etc.) to share with parents. At the same time, parents can relate to these adults as ones who are aware of young people's needs and desires. To avoid confusion, the adult needs to keep each side of the communication confidential and as emotionally objective as possible. Rather than rivals, youth and parents and adult leaders can recognize one another as partners in enhancing mutual growth and fulfillment.

### "thanks. by the way, what am i called—besides 'hey, you'?"

The word used as the title of an adult leader with youth often communicates emotional content which influences youth's initial reaction to the adult, in addition to somewhat shaping the manner in which an adult goes about youth involvement. The word that best encompasses the role presented in this article is COUN-SELOR.

In legal usage, counselor means advocate, i.e., one who is FOR you. In therapeutic circles, the term counselor connotes acceptance and concern. In educational parlance, counselor indicates one who uses skills and insights to assist. So. . . .

Counselor, it's *your* witness!